INTERNATIONAL
PUBLIC
RELATIONS
IN PRACTICE

INTERNATIONAL PUBLIC RELATIONS IN PRACTICE

First Hand Experience of 14 Professionals

Edited by

Margaret Nally

KOGAN PAGE

The masculine pronoun has been used throughout this book. This stems from a desire to avoid ugly and cumbersome language and no prejudice, discrimination or bias is intended.

First published in 1991

Kogan Page Limited
120 Pentonville Road
London N1 9JN
© Margaret Nally, 1991

British Library Cataloguing in Publication Data
A CIP record for this book is available from the British Library.
ISBN 0 7494 0311 X

Typeset by Saxon Printing Ltd., Derby.
Printed and bound in Great Britain by Biddles Ltd., Guildford & King's Lynn.

CONTENTS

Foreword

DOUGLAS SMITH BA, DipCAM, FIPR
Chairman of the PMS Group plc.

One of the founding fathers of the profession in the UK was
Sir Stephen Tallents, first president of the Institute of Public
Relations. He made his name through the Empire Marketing
Board, some of the activity of which must be classed as
'international public relations'. In one sense, therefore, this
important area of communication work could be said to have
been there at the very start.

Certainly, many earlier practitioners in the UK operated on
a global scale — especially those engaged in public relations
during World War II. But then we reverted to a more insular
mood and generally (with a few noble exceptions) concentrated on building up our home markets to become, as we are
now, the largest national public relations group in Europe,
but to the detriment of exploring those wider challenges of
international media and mentalities.

Now we have our hats once again firmly in the international
ring: English has become the business language of Europe,
and the UK the crossroads of much investment into the
European Community from both North America and the Far
East.

This is a magnificent, if somewhat fortuitous, opportunity,
but more of us must develop international skills if the chances
are to be seized. Hence, the importance of this timely book,
contributed by leaders in their respective fields. It should
encourage more to swim in these fascinating waters and,

hopefully, also give our international friends an insight into UK practice.

About the Editor

MARGARET NALLY

Margaret Nally DipCAM, FIPR, CERP started full-time work in public relations in 1955 and has operated in consultancy since that time. Until September 1965, she ran the departments of three advertising agencies, with two short periods in an international consultancy. Since then, she has operated as a solo, independent consultant.

Her work has covered a very broad range but has tended to be primarily in the industrial, business and institutional areas.

Having joined the Institute of Public Relations (IPR) in 1957, she soon began serving on various committees and the Council, and was duly elected a Fellow in 1972. As vice-chairman and then chairman of the Education Committee, she was closely involved in the transfer of public relations education to the newly formed CAM Foundation and instigated the programme in 1974 whereby senior members of the IPR could sit for the CAM Diploma without taking the preliminary examination.

In 1976, she was the first woman president of the IPR and in 1987, the first woman to receive the Stephen Tallents Medal. She also, for a time, held office in and represented the Press and Public Relations branch of the NUJ.

Since the beginning of her public relations work, she has operated for mainland Europe companies marketing in the UK, and for UK companies exhibiting and operating overseas. Since 1976, she has been active with CERP, the European Confederation of Public Relations, has represented the IPR on its Council, served on its Executive Board and been commended for her services. She is currently secretary of the pan-European association, CERP CONSULTANTS.

Two of her three children have followed her into international public relations practice.

Preface

WHY INTERNATIONAL PUBLIC RELATIONS?

International Public Relations in Practice is intended to meet the increasing need for public relations practitioners everywhere to extend the vision and programming of their activities beyond the boundaries of their own country — or even continent.

The term 'global village' is somewhat over quoted by now, but everyone working in communication knows that advances in technology have not only radically changed the opportunities and responsibilities of their work but, also, the scope of all the fields of activity which they support, assist and serve.

All the contributors, leading practitioners in their particular fields, are members of the UK professional body, The Institute of Public Relations; the concept of the book came from the IPR's International Committee. The various chapters, each devoted to a specific theme, show practical knowledge and expertise in using public relations skills and techniques in an international context.

The individual attitudes and approaches of the various contributors come through thus providing a bonus insight into different methodologies and scenarios.

If there is a link or strand which runs through all these crystals of knowledge, it is the need to remember the individual facets. In other words, thinking globally means thinking locally as well.

Acknowledgements

The editor would like to thank all the contributors for the time and support they have generously provided without recompense.

Mike Beard wishes to note that Claire Winterflood and Joanne Graham assisted with his manuscript in their own time and Angela Heylin thanks Janet Simpson for doing the same.

Ann Linscott quoted from a research report on the Japanese market. This was taken from 'The Japanese Market Opportunity', a report by Price Waterhouse marketing consultancy, commissioned by the Opportunity Japan Campaign, an industry-led campaign headed by the Department of Trade and Industry and the Employment Department.

CHAPTER ONE

Organizing the International Operation

ANGELA HEYLIN

Angela Heylin FIPR, FCIM *is chairman and chief executive of Charles Barker, one of the UK's largest communication groups, and also heads a network of 33 affiliated consultancies in 23 countries.*

She is chairman of the Public Relations Consultants Association (PRCA), a founder member of the International Committee of Public Relations Consultants Associations (ICO) and a former trustee of both the Public Relations Education Trust (PRET) and the International Foundation of Public Relations Studies. She was given the public relations industry award for 'Outstanding Contribution to the Industry' in 1988.

Having trained and worked as a secretary, she started her public relations career with El Al Israel Airlines.

ROGER HAYWOOD

Roger Haywood ABC, MCAM, FIPR *is chairman of Roger Haywood Associates Limited, a consultancy which is the European coordinating office for the Worldcom Group, the largest consultancy network in the world, with 60 partners and 100 offices in all major capitals. He chairs both the world organization and the European region.*

He has been marketing and public relations adviser to leading UK and international companies in industries ranging from high technology to financial services and consumer products. His consultancy specializes in national and international communication and is unusual in combining marketing and public relations expertise.

In addition to the 1991 presidency of the IPR, offices he has held include governor of the Communication, Advertising and Marketing Education Foundation (CAM); vice-chairman of the board of management of the Public Relations Consultants Association (PRCA) and vice-chairman of the Chartered Institute of Marketing.

He began his career as a copywriter, moving on to marketing positions and then into international communication.

GAVIN TREVITT

Gavin Trevitt **MIPR** *is currently public relations manager in London for International Maritime Satellite Organization, Inmarsat, an international operation providing global mobile communication via satellite.*

His entire public relations career has been in the international arena, operating in-house, and covering all aspects of public relations, advertising, exhibitions and publicity. He trained and worked as a journalist in Australia and in 1968 moved into public relations as public relations officer to OTC, Australia's international telecommunications carrier.

In 1978, he moved to Washington DC as the first public information officer for Intelsat, the international organization which operates the satellites that carry most of the world's international communication.

Organizing the International Operation

AN ALTERNATIVE APPROACH TO INTERNATIONAL PUBLIC RELATIONS

Angela Heylin

The imminent arrival of a single market of 323 million souls post-1992, the changes in the Eastern bloc, financial deregulation, increased international competition and changing global issues all demand that the public relations industry acts to help management interpret and respond to broader communication needs. Cultural, regulatory, financial media and government relations all vary from one country to the next and public relations practice has to adapt to these local needs and conditions. Thus — think global, act local — is the approach adopted by many companies and organizations in planning communication strategy.

There are currently four main options open to the purchaser of public relations consultancy services across national boundaries. The use of a wholly-owned consultancy network with local offices, generally opened and built up by the parent company and bearing its name, has been the traditional route for many multinationals. More recently, a second type of wholly-owned network has emerged via the acquisition of local agencies and retention of local management and staff.

A third style of networking exists through a lead consultancy taking an equity participation in agencies in other countries, while a fourth option — the creation of a network of independent consultancies — is the choice of many agencies here and abroad which wish to retain ownership of their business while enjoying the benefits of international affiliation. The latter philosophy has advantages which makes it a viable alternative to the wholly-owned network.

A network driven by market forces, covering a total skills mix, provides a tailor-made solution for each client. In major markets, there is more than one consultancy to cover the range of specialities. If the designated consultancy does not have the necessary expertise, its knowledge of the local market is used to refer the client to a consultancy which possesses the required skills. The client, expecting a cost-effective service, thus has access to the best and most appropriate consultancy in the market.

The argument used by wholly-owned networks is that while the levels of public relations sophistication vary between countries, the single-brand offer provides the only guarantee of consistent quality. But surely the ultimate quality control is the threat of dismissal? The client needs a chain in which every link is strong and where, if one link is weak, it can and will be changed — quality through pragmatism rather than ownership.

The alternative network will, of necessity, operate differently from its wholly-owned counterpart in terms of culture and individual contribution. A network of independents means not imposing system, bureaucracy and single culture on individual members. On the contrary, its success depends to some extent on the retention of the differences and on the protection of hard-won success as individual

[20]

companies. Contributions will be demanded from all members — not large financial contributions, for the running costs of the operation should be minimal, but contributions of the creative kind: new services to be offered; knowledge and experience to be shared; introductions to be made; willing and fast support and help for clients in need. However, a network of independent consultancies does need a recognized leader to give it overall direction.

As the international purchaser of public relations services becomes more demanding, more self-sufficient and more sophisticated, the alternative networks that offer flexibility and a bespoke approach will be in a strong position to take advantage of international opportunities.

ARE THE ISSUES CONVERGING?

Roger Haywood

International public relations used to be a specialized branch of the craft. Increasingly, national public relations is becoming a part of the bigger international public relations scene. Today, fewer organizations have a totally domestic perspective — even when they are not operating outside their own national borders. This is because the issues that are concerning people often have a relevance around the world. There is a closing gap in the standards of operation between the industrialized nations and the Third World. Emerging democracies do not want their people treated as second-class citizens and so both the social pressures and legislation move towards higher standards, openness in management, a social responsibility to match profit objectives, and a vision that balances the wider world against personal gain. When it is topical and fashionable to talk about the environment, this is, indeed, an area where the broader responsibilities are increasingly being put ahead of shorter-term profits.

The result of all this 'internationalization' of issues is that these have a greater impact — even on domestic operations. For example, if asbestos is a health hazard in Tennessee, then it is not likely to be acceptable for long in Thailand. If safety guarding is compulsory on factory machinery in Manchester, then how long before it becomes a requirement in Manchuria? If PCBs (polychlorinated biphenyls) are killing marine life in the North Sea then who is going to tolerate them in the South Pacific? But communication is very domestic, so even national organizations have to look carefully at the international scene as it could have a major impact upon the way they work and their acceptability to the key publics upon whom they depend for success.

However, there are many organizations that are international in their operations. In other words, they buy, sell, trade, market, promote, appeal, lobby or communicate in more than one country. What they have all learned is that communication is extremely local and very personal. While some transcontinental messages may be acceptable, most of those that affect people's lives need to be presented to them from a very short range, in a language and style that they can accept, and with an opportunity to debate, challenge, argue and (it is to be hoped) endorse.

For example, everyone wants to turn their television on to hear what the President of the US or of the USSR has to say about the latest international issue. People might accept a company chairman from Turin or Toronto telling them what the year's financial results have been, but they would be less than comfortable about him talking about those local factors that directly affect their working lives. He cannot know enough about their concerns, he has a much bigger scene to supervise and he will be so many levels removed that it is not realistic to envisage any feedback or any interplay of ideas. Fundamentally, if an audience is French it wants a Frenchman to talk to it about those issues and concerns that matter. A vice-president from Virginia will have a difficult job trying to establish a rapport with the workers in Wigan.

What are the international choices? A multinational corporation faces some of the most difficult communication challenges. It can ignore these — many do — and rely on luck for people to understand where the organization is headed

[22]

and what they have to do to make the maximum contribution. Some organizations understand the challenge but then leave the communication in the hands of non-specialists who have to fit this in with all their other responsibilities. This is better than ignoring the problems but is rarely an ideal solution, unless these managers are extremely close to the centre and are very thoroughly briefed, and have some individual communication capabilities.

An alternative can be to get professional communication assistance by recruiting public relations personnel in each country. This can be an effective solution where a proper communication network is established and executives of the right seniority are recruited. These executives also have to be operating at the highest level of national management with a true access into the international communication centre. The reality is that this is very rarely the case. Usually, several layers of local management work hard to make direct communication with the centre impossible. They often resent a non-line manager who is better informed on corporate topics than the line management may be.

Other companies use a local consultancy to provide the communication support. This can also work but may have the limitation that the independent consultancies may not be working to a consistent policy and may not have good communication between themselves. If they are carefully picked, this can be a working solution, but it does require that cross-communication processes between each supporting consultancy are established and that they meet for regular briefings.

By far the most satisfactory solution seems to be to get the highest level of public relations professional help by appointing a consultancy that has an international capacity to match that of the client. This can be an expensive and a less-than-comfortable solution. Each partner in the consultancy network will have a responsibility towards the broader communication effectiveness that may override the shorter-term requirements of local management. Such advice may be correct but may not be locally popular.

There are three main types of international network and each has its plus and minus factors. First, there is the group of companies that has grown organically through the parent opening up an organization where there seemed to be a market need or requirement from their clients. This would include the multinational firms like Burson-Marstellar or Hill & Knowlton.

More recently, a number of networks have arisen that have sprung from one company making strategic acquisitions around the world. In these cases, the local identity of the subsidiaries may be somewhat stronger as they will always be staffed by local people. On the other hand, tight coordination of international objectives does require a lot more work and effort. Examples of companies within this category would be Shandwick, Grey Communications and Omnicom.

A third international option is the network of independent companies which come together to offer a transnational service. This can give the benefit of consultancies owned and operated by the principals; and often picked to be the best of their type in each market. Clearly, the disadvantage can be that the programmes would usually be effected through cooperation rather than direction from the centre. The largest and best-established of this type of partnership is Worldcom.

Groundwork matters most

Whichever route an organization may choose, the same basic disciplines that apply to a domestic programme are still relevant. For example, the current position in each market needs to be clearly understood:

- Who are the key audiences the organization depends upon for success?

- What are their perceptions?

- To what extent do they understand and support the organization?

- Where are there gaps in the communication matrix?

- What improvements need to be made?

From the appraisal of this position, the objectives of the communication activity can be defined. This will also identify the messages that will need to be projected and the means for ensuring effective feedback for management policy-making. Only when these elements are fully clear can the methods be planned to ensure the right solution for the right situation. Finally, the procedures for monitoring the effectiveness and implementing any changes as the campaigns progress can be agreed.

This logical, rational and planned approach to communication needs to be carried out in each country where there are publics of importance.

THE WORLD IS HUGE

Gavin Trevitt

Anyone working in international public relations must keep on reminding themselves that the world represents numbers, variety and complexity almost beyond imagining. It is so easy for one's thoughts to be governed by a subconscious perception of the world which reflects that part of it in which one lives. Constant vigilance is required and it is an advantage to have work colleagues from all over the globe as a reminder of one's own insularity.

With media relations personal contact is best, of course, but very difficult and costly when the territory is global. The next best thing is to use someone local. After all, they know the local ground rules and current issues. Consider using someone from the local branch or sales agency. Local public relations agencies can be satisfactory, particularly for a one-hit announcement or launch, but they are expensive and sometimes difficult — particularly when being recruited from a distance. The telephone can work well, for someone with the right personality, and combined with fax makes a powerful contact-making and contact-keeping tool. However, it is likely to involve working odd hours to keep pace with world time differences.

Media releases and information distribution can be a real headache. For solid news to real-time media (newspapers, radio, television), faxing or telexing a short-list of favourite publications, stations or journalists can work. Telex is still the only reasonably pervasive method of electronic text distribution although the fax is catching up fast. Wire services should be targeted — after all they are set up specifically to distribute news worldwide. Public relations wire services are generally limited in their international coverage and very expensive when stretched beyond their countries or regions. The emergence of specialist press data base services holds some promise for the future.

For now, to distribute non-time-critical information all over the world, particularly if the information contains more than just text, there is, unfortunately, no substitute for a well-tuned mailing list. To ensure it is as accurate as possible, it has to be cleaned regularly. If possible, it should be kept in such a way as to enable selection of specific countries or regions or particular areas of interest. International mail is costly but 'hometown boy makes good' stories work all over the world.

What about language? English is fine most of the time. At Inmarsat, material is produced in four languages: English, French, Russian and Spanish. For every 30,000 English copies, 2,000 are produced in the other languages — and we still run out of the English first. Maybe this example is not totally valid, but it is true that English is the most widely understood language in the world today.

Having said that, it is obviously courteous and much more effective if you express your messages in the language of the intended recipient. This is particularly important at exhibitions and at international business-to-business events. It pays to set out your main messages in the language of the host country and to have at least one person who speaks the language working with you. If that person is a local, so much the better — he will be able to tell you the location of all the best restaurants! As far as news releases are concerned, it is necessary to weigh up the effectiveness of delivering in the local language against the time taken to get translation; and the possibility that undetected inaccuracies may be inadvertently incorporated. With news, time must take precedence.

Exhibitions can be a very useful but very difficult item for the in-house, international public relations person, particularly if the organization does not have a branch or office in the country of the exhibition. Just finding the right exhibition is a challenge when working worldwide. Comprehensive listings are hard to find and exhibition promotion is notoriously ambiguous. In addition to checking on the attendance profile, research among associates and competitors is useful. Best of all, if there is adequate lead time, make a personal check visit.

The practical elements of taking part in the international exhibition circuit require enlisting an experienced operator or operators to deal with design, construction, shipping, installation etc. Final payment on completion of the job can be helpful. The process of taking an exhibition unit in and out of countries, particularly in the developing world, can be very expensive and fraught with hazard. It is necessary to be prepared for 'quaint' local customs and labour practices, and it is often cheaper to scrap the stand/display rather than ship it back. But even this can cause problems with import duties. Local staff should be sought. They will be able to speak the local dialects and know where that missing 'whatsit' can be obtained.

In spite of the problems, exhibitions can be valuable to an international organization. With the right one, the stand can be a regional office for a short time. Given suitable publicity, anyone in the region interested in the organization's business can find the stand easily and make contact. It can also be a base from which to visit them.

CHAPTER TWO

The Corporate Aspect

TIM TRAVERSE-HEALY

Tim Traverse-Healy OBE, DipCAM,
H-FIPR *is an Honorary Professor at the
Universities of Wales and Stirling, Scotland,
and a visiting Professor at the University of
Baylor, Texas. He is a consultant to Corporate Communications plc. Having joined The
Institute of Public Relations in its foundation year, 1948, he has maintained a close
connection, serving as president in 1967–8,
and received the first Stephen Tallents
Medal in 1984. He has operated internationally both in his public relations work and
via his membership of IPRA.*

The Corporate Aspect

One of the professional truisms oft voiced and often heard is that the structure and character of a public relations department should and does reflect the culture and style of the corporation or institution itself. If this is so on a national level, then how much more so it would seem to be the case on an international plane. Perhaps this is because just as the television lens magnifies the nature of its subject, so the very size of the multinational corporate canvas presents to the independent observer, distanced from the scene, a truer vision of the complete picture.

But then, arguably, an international public relations department — or a consultancy for that matter — should not reflect the organization (or clients) it has been created to serve, but rather the job it has to do and thus the various publics with which it has to provide an interface. It has been the author's experience over the past 40 years that, under pressure from the external environment, the department within a corporation that must change its shape, staffing and activities first and more drastically than other staff functions is the public relations unit.

Indeed, distinct patterns have emerged in regard to the handling of international programmes since the publication by the author of the results of a study of 58 multinational companies operating in Europe in 1977 (Traverse-Healy, T.

[31]

(1977) 'Public Affairs Activity by Multinationals in Europe' *IPRA Review* **1**, no. 1, September).

Now, as then, the structures reflect, fundamentally, the definition the particular company applies to public relations and the historical and commercial emphasis of its activities. A concern providing essentially 'services', whether consumer or specialist, organizes itself differently to one providing 'products', be they industrial, consumer durable or 'FMCG' (fast-moving consumer goods). Financial and industrial corporations with production histories organize themselves differently to those commercial concerns presenting a marketing emphasis. Again traditionally, some companies have always tended to maintain internally strong comprehensive staff functions, of which public relations is one, while others have gone the route of having at the centre small yet highly professional units, relying on outside help where and when needed for counsel and assistance.

Even if it were a generalization, it would be true to say that production-orientated corporations, with substantial plant and labour forces, viewed the public relations function as an extension of the chairman or the chief executive's office, part of the machinery of industrial statesmanship and diplomacy. On the other hand, companies with a marketing emphasis, and especially those distributing and selling branded consumer goods, tended to see public relations as part of that process, either helping to create and maintain the overall climate within which sales could be achieved, or, more specifically, a method whereby products and brands could gain additional recognition and acceptance.

Although these distinctions remain visible, changes in thinking and practice have occurred over the last two decades, pressed upon industry and commerce by three forces; forces which have gathered strength since the end of World War II. Briefly, these forces are the public and official demands for more corporate information and greater disclosure; general recognition that a company's actions do impact socially upon others; and acceptance that the stakeholders of an enterprise comprise many more groups other than shareholders and that balancing, or being seen to attempt to balance, the often conflicting interests of these significant groups is a responsibility of modern management — a responsibility ignored at its peril.

Unilever provides, in part, a vivid illustration of this phenomenon. Until the late fifties, it was the operational policy of that company only to promote the brands its various components marketed and not to present the companies that manufactured them. It was certainly not policy (other than in a limited fashion to shareholders) to discuss the corporation behind them. Then, commencing with Van de Bergs, its margarine subsidiary, followed by the mighty United Africa Company and then Lever Brothers, its detergent producer, Unilever began to seek a wider interface with a variety of its publics, albeit continuing to be somewhat reticent regarding corporate information.

Today, the situation is very different. Readiness has replaced reticence and Unilever is prepared to discuss its overall corporate record — its contribution, its performance and its views across its spectrum of interest — openly with any and all. Recognition indeed that the difference between publicity and propaganda on one side, and public relations and information on the other, is the presence — in the process — of truth and concern for the public interest and the existence of genuine dialogue with society.

But apart from these three political and social forces, six trends — sometimes in conflict — are also shaping the nature of public relations activities and the shape of public relations departments. These are:

1. The move within business generally towards rationalization, the cutting down of numbers at the centre, the devolution of authority and the decentralization of operations, and the creation of autonomous profit centres.

2. The development of international matrix management, resulting in cross-border product command and control, as distinct from country-based direction.

[33]

3. The fact that not all multinational corporations market global brands; many, arguably more, market brands with distinct local national characteristics.

4. Conversely, the political, social, and commercial issues which drive the public affairs programmes and demand a public relations response, are not only often interrelated in themselves, but more often than not are global in development and expression.

5. Paradoxically, while corporations are 'decentralizing' on the outside, information and the media of communication are 'centralizing' in the sense that facts, figures, and opinions are shared from data bases worldwide with the speed of electronic sight and sound.

6. Furthermore, all the signs are that over the next two decades, as a result of newly developing technology, readily available, the focus is moving away from institutions and mass communication towards individuals and speedy personalized direct response activity.

In the light of the foregoing, what seems to be the consensus of the opinions of experienced consultants and in-house practitioners as regards the organization of public relations activity internationally? Certain axioms have emerged:

1. The credit for creating and maintaining sound external relationships and the blame for having poor corporate public relations cannot, and should not, be removed from the senior company line executive responsible for a particular country, territory, or product range.

2. Internally, a distinction can be made between central corporate public policy and the local expression of that policy in local public relations contact-and-convince programmes.

3. The public is 'out there', not at Head Office, and therefore 'out there' is where the action has to be.

If these axioms are accepted, then it follows that a number of checks and balances need to be put in place to ensure that policies are implemented and effective programmes are created, mounted, and evalued.

AT THE CENTRE

- Clear policies need to exist (and be updated) as regards the corporation's identity, image, culture and ethics.
- Clear positions need to be established regarding issues of public or group interest.
- Strategies need to be articulated identifying target audiences, messages, tone, stance and importance of programme.
- Communication objectives and themes in support of the corporation's missions and business plans need to be determined.
- Benchmarks for evaluation purposes need to be agreed.
- Budgets and controls have to be set.
- Systems governing advance planning approval, post-programme review and audits must be installed.
- Reporting and accountability requirements need to be approved.
- Procedures for appointing local outside helpers need to be established.
- Restrictions as to subjects and targets need to be simply and clearly spelt out, and referral procedures mutually agreed.
- The line responsibility and the authority for representing the corporation in a particular country, territory, and market have to be anchored with a nominated executive having regard to possible overlap and local problems arising where more than one facility, area of corporate activity, or product line is present.
- Resources to service the operational requirements of the various programmes as regards information flow and materials have to be made available.

- Facilities to educate, and train, the various corporate executives involved or likely to be involved at grass roots level need to be established.

Irrespective of whether the home office is in New York, London, Paris or Tokyo and the host countries number two or two times twenty, the above principles remain substantially the same. Fundamentally the line manager concerned responds and reports in the normal fashion either directly to his chief executive's office or via the designated line of command — which might be via international territory, area, regional or even product line senior management. What is essential, however, is that, in parallel, all reports in this context also flow to the corporate head of public relations. In large concerns, this might be via a regional public relations executive and an international public relations manager.

AT COUNTRY LEVEL

- Local strategies, plans and programmes need to be created.

- Machinery has to be developed to implement the agreed programmes. This could involve the appointment on to the staff of the necessary professionals or the retention of local consultants and agencies.

- Corresponding reporting, control and evaluation systems, and training and facilities need to be established.

The pros and cons of on-staff, in-house appointments as distinct from the employment of outside consultancies and agencies have been thoroughly aired, as have the competing claims of wholly-owned consultancy chains, federations, or loose associations. Obviously, corporate management has to weigh up a number of considerations in this regard. These include:

- the corporation's overall level of excellence and experience in this particular field of endeavour;

[36]

- the knowledge and expertise of each local management in this regard;

- the nature of the local programme and the particular issues and specialisms involved;

- the extent to which the programme is likely to maintain constancy or progressively change in character and content;

- the competitive situation;

- the structure, customs, and decision-making process of the particular country;

- the time frame involved;

- the corporate culture and policy over staff progression and ambition;

- the desire to develop internally an ongoing knowledge base;

- the local professional recruitment situation, the availability of talent, and the reputation and experience of the local consultancy profession.

But what is often presented as a controversy situation, between appointments in-house or the use of external help, should not in reality be so. The sophisticated corporation has long since learnt to apply the following criteria:

- How best can the centre ensure policy, planning, budgetary control and standards of performance locally?

- Can, as has been proven elsewhere, one of the consultancy linkages, wholly-owned or otherwise, do this efficiently and cost-effectively?

- Or, in our case, would we be best served by staffing up at the centre and perhaps also at regional level?

- Do all or only some of our local components need to have public relations professionals or could local agencies be retained?

- Chemistry and creativity apart, does a particular consultancy or agency chain have experience of special relevance to our current needs?

- Or would we be better served by selecting the 'best' consultancy in each country, irrespective of their ownership and linkages?

- What do the cost comparisons of the different formulae indicate?

- Importantly, what arrangement will the local leader and organization feel most comfortable with?

- And is there present a consultancy with which the local manager and his colleagues will be able to relate?

In the event that a decision is taken to retain local national consultancies then a tried method is for the local corporate management to submit their short-list; for the centre to have the facility to delete names or add the names of those agencies they would also like to see considered; and then to have the local management make the final choice, following investigations, presentations, and visitations. By this method, the centre exercises a degree of control over professional standards and the local unit has a sense of commitment to the agency chosen.

Assuming that the foregoing methodology has been applied, then there remain only three additional dimensions that an international, transnational, multinational corporation, should ponder.

1. Effective public relations policies and programmes depend on accurate, timely information and sound intelligence. For whatever reasons, local reports from within are not always well based or correctly framed. It has ever been so. If the issues involved are of sufficient importance or urgency to the corporation, then the centre might opt to create a second, independent, external line of report and counsel available only to itself. A second look results from knowledge and investment and such validation is rarely wasted.

2. The recruitment, training, and career development of in-house professionals should be overseen by the centre in the corporate interest.

3. Evaluating, measuring, and auditing the effectiveness of local programmes, including the use of opinion and attitudinal research, is a management function over which the centre should have complete control. Otherwise, how can it discharge its corporate stewardship responsibilities?

Fifteen years back, The Conference Board (a well-known international 'peer group' association) published a report (No. 679) entitled *The search for an optimum external relations structure*. Essentially, it addressed the question of 'decentralization' versus 'centralization'. It is submitted that the foregoing review of what is arguably now recognized as 'best practice' goes some way towards resolving that question.

But perhaps a sign of progress is that a group of six academics, led by Professor Grunig of Maryland University, has embarked upon a six-year project, funded by the professional body, which aims to answer the following two questions:

1. How and to what extent does the practice of public relations contribute to the bottom line?

2. What are the characteristics of an excellent in-house department or external consultancy?

The author would like to believe that if the characteristics of 'excellence' implicit in the second question are found to be present in an operation then it will be that much easier to answer the first question positively. Furthermore, it is to be hoped that if the methodology suggested in this chapter were applied to the organization of international public relations then 'excellence' would follow and the resultant enhancement of the 'bottom-line' could be simply proved if not readily obvious for all to see.

Note: This chapter has been adapted from an address by the author to The Management Group (a meeting group for managers) in London, in January 1990.

CHAPTER THREE

Financial Public Relations in a Global Context

ALAN MACDONALD

Alan Macdonald MA, MIPR is head of group corporate communications at Midland Group, which he joined in 1979 as senior public relations officer for Midland Bank International.

He was previously a director of Galitzine and Partners, the European coordinating office of the International Public Relations Group, and also worked in parliamentary and governmental affairs consultancy, and for J Walter Thompson.

He joined Citibank as a graduate trainee, becoming advertising coordinator for the UK and Ireland.

Born in Malta, he has an MA in law from University College, Oxford, and is a member of the Royal Institute of International Affairs.

He contributed the chapter on international dimensions in the CAM Handbook of Financial Public Relations *(1989, Heinemann).*

Financial Public Relations in a Global Context

The internationalization of financial markets has transformed the communication needs, risks and opportunities for participants in those markets. This phenomenon affects all major manufacturing and service companies that do business overseas — not just the stockbrokers and merchant banks which act for them.

Public relations work in the financial arena is a specialized job which requires knowledge of financial institutions and processes, as well as of the financial media. In the case of international activity, a similar understanding of financial markets in other countries is necessary.

When operating across different time zones, often in different languages, timing and wording are even more important than when working in a single market. But these are, after all, key requirements for a public relations professional in every country and every specialization.

CURRENT MEDIA DEVELOPMENTS

Accompanying the increase in coverage of financial affairs in the UK national press and television has been the growth in overseas coverage — particularly from the US and Japan, reflecting their central role as world financial markets. The *Financial Times* now has 20 full bureaux overseas (besides superstringers), with New York, Washington and Tokyo staffed to handle the volume of financial and economic news.

The *Financial Times* international edition is now printed in Germany, France, the US and Japan, and sells more than 100,000 copies. The *Wall Street Journal*'s European edition sells more than 50,000 copies and the Asian edition nearly 40,000 copies. These newspapers and, to a lesser extent, the *International Herald Tribune* have had a much bigger impact on the globalization of news and its treatment than the clutch of cross-border magazines which preceded them. The circulations of the two most financially influential, *Institutional Investor* and *Euromoney*, appear to have peaked.

An even greater change has been seen in electronic publishing, with little green screens replacing hard-copy printers. Agency copy is much more than raw material for tomorrow's newspapers. Now the international news agencies — Reuters, AP-Dow Jones, Knight-Ridder — transmit to dealers' desks and to the offices of financial decision-makers throughout the world. They can all see the same headline within seconds of the story breaking, and increasingly refer to newspapers for comment, rather than news.

The latest advances have been in television, where transfrontier direct broadcasting by satellite is established as an alternative to terrestrial and cable. America's Cable News Network, which gives a high proportion of its air time to US business and financial news, has improved its overseas coverage. NHK (Japan Broadcasting Corporation) has a daily direct feed from London. Both have link-ups with Channel 4's *Business Daily*.

Financial information of general news value can be transmitted by satellite and broadcast live or semi-live simultaneously across one or more continents.

O Globo, based in Rio de Janeiro, has the largest audience of any television company in the world, with an appetite for news nearly as voracious as for 'telenovela' soap operas. A British banker door-stopped emerging from a debt-rescheduling meeting in the International Monetary Fund building in Washington might find himself on a specialist financial slot in the UK and cable television in the US but, by courtesy of *O Globo*, on prime time news throughout half of South America.

CORPORATE IDENTITY

Any organization operating internationally has to decide how it wants to be seen in each market in which it conducts its business. The monolithic approach has particular appeal to consumer goods manufacturers — whether the reason is economy of scale in the production of promotional material or the endorsement benefit of identifying distinct products with the strength of the parent's name. These considerations apply with particular force where recognition of corporate name and linkage to the product range may assist acceptance by the investment community.

There may, however, be clear advantages in being seen as a member of the local community rather than as an alien invader. For instance, in banking, it is rare to find a successful retail banking operation which trades under a foreign name. The majority of UK and Japanese banks in California kept the name of the bank they acquired to exploit the domestic potential. Equally, the only way for a foreign bank to be profitable in Germany is for it to submerge its own national identity and appear to be a German bank.

These considerations apply to a greater or lesser extent wherever in the world banks have offices. The monolithic approach favoured by the US banks is usually the right one in major financial centres which are linked one to another by the confluence of their markets. Foreign exchange is traded on a single global market, with the book passed from Tokyo to London to New York around the clock (and with windows for Sydney, Hong Kong, and San Francisco).

[45]

ADVERTISING

Although advertising is properly regarded as a separate discipline from public relations, in the case of financial advertising — particularly overseas, where there may be no established agency relationship — it is often an integral part of the public relations role.

Horror stories abound of English-language copy appearing in vernacular media and of space booked on national holidays or in defunct publications or the wrong ones. The *Straits Times* in Singapore has frequently been the willing recipient of bookings intended for the *Business Times*, a quite separate newspaper.

Although perfectly respectable transnational campaigns can be created, they must be conceived from the start as such, taking into account local factors, and not just as add-ons to a domestic media schedule. Such campaigns are better suited to cross-border publications, notably the European and Asian editions of the *International Herald Tribune* and *Wall Street Journal*. But these, and the limited number of international magazines, appeal principally to US citizens and employees of US organizations.

There have been standard advertisements placed in indigenous media around the world — Japanese banks have been notable culprits — which have almost certainly done the perpetrators more harm than good. Quaint and alien themes and translations made in the country of origin deter, rather than encourage, business relationships.

There are some excellent examples of foreign campaigns taken up by local agencies, but these have been adaptations, not just translations. The ideal may be to provide local managers with the brief to the main agency and each advertisement in the series but to give them as much leeway as they need, allowing separate campaigns where local circumstances dictate.

Overseas financial advertising requires a significant financial outlay if it is to have any kind of impact against the weight of advertising of indigenous advertisers. A clear case can be made for advertising an opening, acquisition or name change to the financial community and for placing tombstones recording financial transactions. But even the value of advertising the parent's annual results should be carefully weighed.

In some countries, there are written or unwritten rules about the size and position, as well as the wording, of financial advertisements to ensure that they comply with the norm established by or for the local players. Generally, educating local managers in a fuller understanding of the public relations opportunities and responsibilities may prove a better investment.

FINANCIAL COMMUNITY RELATIONS

For any financial institution, whose competitors are usually also its customers and often its regulators, fitting into its local community is a necessity rather than a preference. For non-financial companies, there may also be value in a raised profile within the financial community.

Planned and sustained activity, which might include serving on committees, drafting technical papers to educate supervisors or regulators, speaking to study groups, writing articles for financial periodicals and giving evidence to legislative committees, should be regarded as essential duties for the officer in charge of the local operation or for the chief financial officer of a non-financial company. Visits of the chairman and other head office 'firemen' should be seen in this broader context, and should not be restricted to contact with managers and customers.

It is in this area that international sponsorship can prove effective, rather than just reaching customers. Sponsorship can act as a short cut in creating a place for the sponsor within the local community, both in the sense of the association through the nature of the event and in the sense of useful shoulders that can be rubbed while the event is being planned and organized. Non-financial companies should consider the benefit of including financial guests for corporate entertainment opportunities when the event is in progress.

Preparing the ground in these ways can make a significant difference to the acceptance of a foreign company's business plans, including licence applications, acquisitions, disposals and lay-offs. At the very least, it should ensure that the local manager knows which officials, legislators and other opinion-formers to speak to.

EMPLOYEE COMMUNICATION

In communicating with staff in overseas locations, it should be remembered that the local manager will be regarded by customers, counterparties and authorities as the plenipotentiary of his organization in every particular. He will, therefore, require information at the same time as it is released to the media on any major development, regardless of whether or not his divisional superior in head office is affected by it. This usually calls for a central information system, whether by electronic mail, multi-telexing or fax transmission.

On developments affecting his operations directly, he should expect to receive a call, preferably from the manager to whom he reports, before the news breaks and before he receives the release. It is sometimes difficult for local managers to understand that they cannot receive price-sensitive information in advance, which this courtesy should correct.

Communication with management and staff of an acquired company are a particular consideration. The basic rule is only to communicate in the first instance through their own top management who will communicate in their own language and their own style. Material should be immediately available to enable them to present information on your business — its history, organization and standing — to their own staff. But excessive familiarization may instil more despondency than delight.

USING PUBLIC RELATIONS AGENCIES

Public relations agencies can prove valuable to overseas offices which cannot justify employing the requisite in-house skills. This is particularly true in the case of financial work, although practitioners are scarce outside the world financial centres. The costs can be high, particularly in Tokyo and New York where £7,000 might be regarded as a minimum monthly retainer, so a clear understanding of what is required for this outlay is necessary.

The minimal requirement is that the agency can turn a news release round and fax major news items to head office immediately. Whatever their intentions, whether or not they have the expertise, overseas offices are unlikely to accomplish even this basic requirement themselves unless they have an individual seriously dedicated to the task.

A public relations agency should also be able to seek opportunities for interviews for the local manager, specialists and head office visitors. This requires briefing on issues and rehearsing questions and answers, and should amount to more than just a diary function.

A consultancy can also be a useful source of political and governmental information and can advise expatriate managers on local procedures and protocol. It should also be able to assist the manager in his community role — both financially and more generally — by suggesting contacts, by making introductions, and by looking for external opportunities generally.

The ideal consultant is likely to be a local national or of the nationality of the colonial power. Apart from cultural considerations, expatriates usually stay for too short a time to have the necessary experience.

INVESTOR RELATIONS

Whether or not a firm decision has been made to list a

company's shares on an overseas stock market, the public relations practitioner should be aware of the benefits and constraints, and should prepare the way for the eventuality in its relations with the local financial community (see above).

An overseas stock market quotation can significantly raise the profile of the listed company, magnifying news, whether good or bad. Similar considerations apply to shelf registrations for yankee bonds (US dollar bond issues by foreign companies in the domestic market). The prescriptive disclosure requirements in the US have led foreign companies issuing bonds to detail more in their annual reports to bring them in line with their required report form 20-Fs, filed annually with the Securities and Exchange Commission. As these documents are available to analysts and journalists, they would otherwise be providing less information to their shareholders at home than to overseas audiences.

The listing itself should be exploited to the full. No better opportunity exists to present an organization on its own terms to a financial community. A listing can enhance awareness of a company's products or services, and create a base for local acquisitions. In European countries, raising visibility may in itself be a sufficient cause for the exercise. A presentation to a joint audience of stockbrokers, analysts, institutional fund managers, customers and press, followed by a reception — at which they are handed an information pack containing the prospectus — is the standard practice.

The opportunity genuinely to broaden the shareholder base is much greater in the more liquid markets of the US and Japan, whether through issuing new shares or offering existing shares. The continuing requirement for quarterly reporting in the US and for translation of routine material in Japan are onerous and expensive, so no company should contemplate a listing on their stock exchanges purely for publicity purposes.

In Japan, companies are advised to place themselves safely in the hands of their sponsoring securities house to ensure that they conform to local customs. The normal pattern would be briefings for the Press and analysts, in addition to a series of meetings with individual institutions to encourage them to invest, concluding with a 'mega-reception' in a Tokyo hotel.

In the US, the communication plan does not necessarily depend on which stock exchange has been selected for the quotation or on whether a full listing has been sought or an offering of US depository receipts (a repackaging of existing shares). The norm might be a roadshow to New York, Boston, Chicago, San Francisco and Los Angeles, with a meeting in each for security analysts (from brokerage firms and investing institutions). The media may be invited to these (to fulfil the simultaneous disclosure requirements). There are usually separate meetings with money managers. Investment bank advisers have a less upfront role than in Japan, but are the best route for accessing institutional investors.

The placing of shares on an overseas bourse, a takeover of an overseas quoted company or the buyout of minority shareholders can give rise to a considerable continuing responsibility for presenting to and answering questions from the financial press, analysts, fund managers, shareholders and, in the US, arbitrageurs (raiders who buy in anticipation of a move by a real predator). Apart from making regular visits, it is necessary to offer a local information point for news releases and to be ready to deal with eventualities arising from adverse brokers' circulars and from lawsuits, including class actions from groups of litigants.

Relations with the credit-rating agencies — Moody's and Standard & Poor's are the most prominent — should aim to minimize the impact of bad news. Regradings can affect the cost of borrowing, as well as influencing the ability to raise new equity capital. Rating agencies should receive news releases at the same time as the Press and be contacted directly on any major development. Notice is given of changes, so press spokesmen should be put on alert to take questions arising from downgradings.

CRISIS MANAGEMENT

The instant feedback from overseas of adverse or inaccurate

[51]

coverage is essential. The rumour giving rise to the run on Continental Illinois in Chicago arose in Tokyo. Speculation based on overseas developments can create a false market in a company's shares, because of the difficulty in denying them when the facts may not be immediately known.

When there is a false, misleading or exaggerated report that a company has closed down, given up a line of business, made a major loss or is guilty of criminal activity, it will not just be necessary to arrange a correction with the offending publication, but also to provide the correct information to other media, the authorities and clients. In the case of quoted companies, clarification may be sought by the local stock exchange.

Where the inaccurate story is sourced to agency copy or to an accurate report of remarks by a third party, the publication may well decline to run a correction. The only answer may be to issue another story on the subject in question, thus demonstrating the inaccuracy of the previous report. An alternative may be an interview with the local manager. The London correspondent may be a good route for a correction, whether or not he perpetrated the error in the first place.

A serious rumour or leak or a real disaster may necessitate a more elaborate series of measures involving all employees in contact with the public. It is vital under these circumstances that any new developments are communicated instantly to all centres affected. Close contact with the Foreign Office in London, and through the British embassy in the country concerned, with the relevant authorities in that country and with the foreign embassy in London may be required. Great sensitivity is necessary when a commercial organization is caught in diplomatic crossfire as a result of its operations in such countries as South Africa, Libya and Argentina. This is particularly so when its core domestic business comes under attack from a political, religious or other pressure group.

FOREIGN CORRESPONDENTS

Of the 1,000 foreign correspondents in London, some 70

exclusively cover financial news. Many others include business in their general news coverage. There is no such concentration elsewhere in the world, even in the US, where they are split between New York and Washington. The key financial correspondents, except for the Americans (who have their own organization), all belong to the Foreign Press Association in London. Associate membership is available for public relations practitioners.

The Central Office of Information (COI) has a London correspondents' service, dividing them into groups covering finance, defence, and science and technology (as well as culture). The COI organizes visits throughout the UK, including two or three a month for the financial group. It also arranges introductory programmes for newly arrived correspondents and occasional group visits for non-financial specialists wishing to know more about the City or business.

Of the financial specialists, *Wall Street Journal* and AP-Dow Jones should be seen as international rather than American, and their UK penetration should be taken into account. Agence France Presse also ranks as an international medium. Reuters should, of course, be regarded for its overseas coverage in addition to its dominant position within the UK financial community.

The German contingent is even more in evidence than the American, with *Handelsblatt, Frankfurter Allgemeine Zeitung* and *Borsen Zeitung* regularly reporting UK financial news. *Die Welt* is more concerned with economics, with thinner coverage on business matters. From Switzerland, *Neue Zuricher Zeitung* should be included for any major financial announcements. Of the Japanese media, the Jiji Press wire service and *Nihon Keizai Shimbun*, with its financial, industrial and English-language affiliates, have strong bureaux.

There are good opportunities for television and radio coverage. American television has an insatiable appetite for market comment against a dealing-room background. American broadcasters rely more on their sources to comment on the news than is the norm for UK television. This fact can prove of great benefit for companies active in the US. Any organization that can offer interviewees speaking in the language of the television company concerned — and this also applies to the BBC Overseas Service — has a considerable competitive advantage.

NEWS RELEASES

Particular care has to be taken with the wording of releases intended for consumption in more than one country, especially where translation is necessary. This is a powerful argument for writing in simple English and for avoiding legal terms — not a consideration that legal and corporate finance advisers tend to take into account.

Where there is a joint release in two centres, for example for a takeover or joint venture, it may be preferable to have two separate versions rather than attempting a series of compromises. An alternative may be to place different quotations in otherwise identical releases or to switch paragraphs or the order of company names. Translations should always be made in the country of destination by translators accustomed to writing for the Press and be checked by an individual within the client organization with the financial or technical knowledge to do so.

Special attention must be paid to the wording of the first sentence (and, to a lesser extent, the headline), as this will determine the headline on news printers and screens, which will have a significant impact on the tone of the coverage and how the story is picked up, passed on and used around the world. No release should be drafted to build up gradually to its real point if there is to be any control of how the news is carried on the newswires.

DISTRIBUTION

The three principal routes for issuing news releases internationally — and all three should be exploited — are newswires, foreign correspondents and distribution in the country concerned. It is also possible to telex or fax overseas media directly as an alternative. Direct electronic input is not yet an option, although the London Stock Exchange's Topic service is received by the international wire services in London.

Any story of major significance will be carried on the wires worldwide. In Japan, for example, economic and financial news on AP-Dow Jones can run on Kyodo and items on Reuters can run on Jiji Press, translated into Japanese. The wires will usually fulfil the disclosure requirement in the US, where simultaneous release is stipulated, rather than a requirement to advise stock exchanges in advance.

It is still worthwhile, however, to issue the full release in overseas centres, as Reuters, AP-Dow Jones and other agencies rarely carry stories in full. In the US, to ensure that the full version is transmitted to all major media across the continent, the only answer is to release through PR News Wire (in New York) and the Business Wire (in San Francisco).

Unless confidentiality is essential, it is important to set the release up for issue in overseas centres, including translation, ahead of time. Otherwise, the full version will be too late to compete with the newswire versions.

Where there is no public relations agency or competent local management or partner (eg in an acquired company), a release can be telexed or faxed to key publications in that country, but they will only accept foreign language releases if they contain very important news. Universal News Services (UNS) offers a commercial overseas service, with a scale of charges for reaching continents and individual countries.

TIMING

Timing is a critical consideration. Drafters and approvers of press releases should be made aware that meeting deadlines may be more important then refining content. It is necessary to determine priorities. Which country is the most important? When are the media deadlines? What are the opening hours of the stock exchanges affected?

With the Company News Service of the International Stock Exchange in London, it is normal practice to release between 7.30 am and 9 am (whether under embargo or not). This will not present a problem for the eastern and western seaboards of the US if preparations are made to release early in New York, preferably by 7.30 am, when Dow Jones opens, and in time for the opening of the New York and American stock exchanges and of the electronic over-the-counter market (Nasdaq) at 9.30 am.

In the case of a story originating in the US, even if released after the close of the principal US exchanges at 4 pm, it would still be possible to make the final editions of the UK press, if it is an important enough story. After 7 pm or 8 pm London time, primary responsibility for handling a US/UK story normally passes to the New York bureau of the *Financial Times*.

With a price-sensitive story, it is advisable to inform the specialist correspondents of the quality dailies after the stock exchange has closed that there is a major story coming, without giving any details. They can then decide whether to stay late or put their newsdesks on notice to alert them at home when the story breaks. If the news is good, it is clearly an advantage for it to be covered by specialists; that way it will probably command more space. If the news if bad, there is a greater risk of inaccuracy resulting from lack of time or knowledge on the newsdesk.

In the case of a story originating in the Far East, where that market is considered of higher priority than the UK, it may be preferable to release during their working day, as long as it is issued after it is too late for the front and back pages of the *Financial Times*, which can still take a major story up to 1 am in the slip edition.

If the item justifies it, it can be picked up on the 5.30 am LBC financial slot, the 6 am BBC Radio news and the 6.45 am BBC *Today* financial slot. So, to be on the safe side, the best expedient is to prepare to transmit to the exchange at 7 am when the company news service opens.

The normal time for press conferences and interviews in Japan and Hong Kong is the early to mid-afternoon, though Australia and Singapore follow the UK style more closely of morning news gathering and afternoon writing. But, for a major development which is too price sensitive for calling a press conference in advance, it is still feasible to call a conference at no notice for the late afternoon in Hong Kong.

In all these centres, it is quite possible to release to coincide with London — 7 am in London is 3 pm in Hong Kong. Even 9 am, if (say) there is a board meeting to give final sign-off at 8 am, allows release at 5 pm in Hong Kong, which is not too late. In Japan, many national and regional dailies publish separate morning and evening editions; the deadline for the nationals is around 12 noon for evening editions, but 1 am for the morning, or an hour later for major news stories.

A danger of late release, however, is that the Press is more likely to react to the versions of the story on the wire services. At best, these may be based on the official release; at worst, they may rely on an external source such as a government department, rating agency or analyst. Another problem with late release is distribution. The latest reliable hand-delivery time in London is 4.30 pm. So the combination of direct input to the London Stock Exchange, reading headlines, faxing and UNS will be necessary to achieve fast release after this time.

To stand a good chance of news being carried the following day in continental Europe, a release should be issued in London by 9 am if it is to be translated and issued that day. Dailies in West Germany require receipt of releases by around noon. The latest time for filing from London is 1 pm for most purposes, though hot news can be accommodated up to 6 pm on most papers.

NATIONAL DIFFERENCES

In seeking to handle financial public relations in overseas centres, full account must be taken of local practices. In the US, for example, reporters do not often insert their own editorial opinions into copy, relying instead on quoting a number of different sources to build up a story. This method presents good opportunities for public relations practitioners, since they can put forward their clients as market commentators and, if they are sufficiently assertive and skilful, create attention for them out of proportion to the size of the organization. But spokesmen have to proceed with extreme care, establishing ground rules before a conversation begins, or it may all be used on the record.

To understand press relations in Japan it is necessary to understand the press club system. There are some 400 clubs, each covering its own specific area, including government ministries, trade associations and political parties, which normally only make official announcements to an organized gathering of the members. News releases have to be issued through the appropriate club, for example the Bank of Japan club for banking news and the Tokyo Stock Exchange club for securities. To distribute a release through a press club, permission has to be sought two days in advance from the club chairman. If it carries an embargo he has to agree the date and time.

Other than the trade journals and magazines outside the system, the Japanese media do not take a news release at face value, but contact the issuer or some other source for confirmation. To be sure that it will be covered, it is necessary to choose one newspaper and give it an exclusive interview. Unless familiar with the company concerned and the economy and financial system in which it operates, a reporter would not feel comfortable in interviewing its representatives, so it is vital to foster relationships with several reporters on each national daily.

In Hong Kong, the Chinese press will print releases often more or less word for word as long as they are translated into Cantonese. But if there is a press conference it is essential to invite the Chinese as well as the English-language media. If they are not invited, they may choose not to run the story unless it represents bad news.

On the other hand, in Singapore, there are not enough press representatives to justify a financial press conference. The best plan is to talk directly to the *Business Times* (Singapore) and to issue a release to the others, including the *Business Times* (Malaysia).

In West Germany, business news stories are generally written in a neutral show-the-figures way. Consistent with this style, quotes from company spokesmen are normally written in indirect speech. By contrast, editorial commentaries, based on the personal opinion of the author, can be more controversial than would be expected in the US or UK. But, in many ways, the German press is becoming more Anglo-Saxon in approach, with more flexible deadlines and less reliance on embargoes to cope with the pressures of the results conference season.

Space does not permit a lengthier dissertation on national quirks, customs and characteristics — financial and otherwise. The understanding of this lasting cultural dimension continues to determine success in the operation of public relations internationally, just as much as the ability to keep pace with fast-moving global information and communication developments.

CHAPTER FOUR

Crisis Management: Planning and Coping Internationally

KATE GRAHAM

Kate Graham MIPR *spent more than twelve years with the international company, Occidental Petroleum, eight as public affairs officer. During that time, she dealt with the media aspects of several offshore incidents and was responsible for the press response to the Piper Alpha disaster.*

Since 1988 she has specialized in press relations and crisis management, undertaking consultancy and staff training for the majority of North Sea operators, as well as numerous other organizations.

Crisis Management: Planning and Coping Internationally

COPING WITH CRISIS

1988 will long be remembered as the year of the crisis. Bold newspaper headlines, lengthy editorials and graphic photographs describing tragedies, most of which we thought simply could not happen, appeared with distressing regularity. In fact, the latter part of the 1980s will, I hope, never be equalled for the long list of disasters which occurred during those few years — Zeebrugge, Kings Cross, Clapham, Lockerbie, British Midland, Hillsborough, Bradford and Piper Alpha — a catalogue of disaster which resulted in the loss of hundreds of lives and which had a profound effect on industry, commerce and sport, not only in the UK but also, worldwide.

In addition to these, we continue to be bombarded by the views of others. We have been under threat from salmonella, listeria and legionnaires disease. We have been advised not to consume eggs, soft cheeses and beef.

Even some fizzy H_2O was taboo for a while — and because of some rather sick-minded individuals, from time to time it becomes somewhat risky to feed your tiny offspring baby foods. The fact is that crises surround us daily, affecting many individuals in a variety of ways.

'Crises occur elsewhere — we really won't be involved.' 'Let's face it, statistically it's very unlikely that it will ever happen to this organization.' I would suggest that these two statements have been repeated many times in company boardrooms. However, whether as employee or employer you wish to write off the entire topic of crisis management on the basis of the assumption 'it can't happen to me' then so be it. I just do not envy the person who finds himself in the unfortunate position of having to be company spokesperson in the event of a crisis occurring.

A crisis is a time of immense stress, emotion and hostility. It is a time for prompt action by skilled specialists so that control can be established from the outset. Lack of preparation coupled with an inability to take charge of a situation can rapidly turn a controllable crisis into an uncontrollable disaster.

NEWS MANAGEMENT

A difficult facet of crisis management is undoubtedly that of news management. Dealing with a news-hungry reporter certainly differs from talking on a day-to-day basis with a reasonable, friendly specialist or features writer. How do you cope when someone screams at you, 'Why were those people killed'?

In July 1988, I was public affairs officer at Occidental Petroleum. On the 6th, from 10pm onwards I found myself trying to cope with an onslaught from the world's press.

My press response staff and colleagues worked round the clock for days on end. Literally thousands of phone calls were handled during the early stages of the Piper Alpha disaster.

There were more than 150 media representatives from all corners of the world present at Dr Hammer's press conference on Friday, 8 July — only 36 hours after the explosion onboard the platform. Media presence was sustained at a very high level for several weeks.

In the aftermath the question so often asked by many bewildered people is 'How did it happen?'. There is seldom a straightforward answer to such a question. Lengthy, in-depth enquiries and the testimony of experts and witnesses are usually required.

Zeebrugge, Kings Cross, Piper Alpha, Clapham, Lockerbie and the British Midlands crash — all had one thing in common; immediately, the public and the media wanted to know what had happened. For several weeks that was the case with Piper Alpha and the involvement of a multinational company ensured that public and media attention were worldwide.

Every incident has been different and the level of response from the organization involved has also varied considerably. One thing is certain, however, when a tragedy occurs, public and media attention is focused on the company concerned.

It is a mistake for any company to issue speculative information during the early stages of a disaster. Conversely, it is absolutely crucial that factual information is imparted to the outside world as soon as possible.

Most large companies do have designated spokespeople and it is their responsibility to handle the barrage of questions which always follows such incidents.

The clock cannot be turned back. Once an incident has occurred, the responsibility for informing the public via the media rests squarely on the shoulders of the company concerned.

That company must be prepared to answer to the best of its ability the obvious questions which arise.

When I read that 'a company spokesperson was unavailable for comment' I know that an open invitation has just been issued to the media to pursue their line of questioning by any means, fair or foul. The result will invariably be inaccurate, speculative reporting which bears no resemblance to the truth. In such circumstances, however, can we honestly blame the media?

Let us look at the difference between the Pan Am and the British Midland air incidents. Both companies had to deal with the onslaught of the press and yet the outcome was very different.

It could be said that Pan Am's position as an international operator involved wider responsibility than that of British Midland. However, lack of information and a dire shortage of constructive comments from Pan Am resulted in an immense amount of speculative information appearing in the newspapers. On the other hand, British Midland's spokesman provided factual information at an early stage, thereby combating to a greater extent the harm that can be done by making no valid comment.

British Rail have also avoided much of the criticism levelled at London Transport by the press and the public by announcing their acceptance of liability and their intention to arrange prompt payment of compensation.

At Occidental, every effort was made to release factual information regularly, backed up by diagrams, photographs and video footage whenever possible. The question of compensation was also handled expeditiously. Press coverage worldwide was immense and a reasonable proportion was fairly accurate.

Controversial food issues continue to emerge. Cast your minds back to the salmonella scare. Although loss of life was not involved, many small businesses paid a heavy price, even though Edwina Currie did clarify what she meant in her initial statement. The fact remains that her explanation may have occurred a bit late in the day for a number of British egg producers.

Public awareness of health matters is on the increase. Owing to public interest in natural foods, the environment and healthy living, we are very likely to see more scares coming to the surface.

CAN YOU COPE?

How can companies prepare for a crisis? I believe that the most important first step is to assess the potential for a crisis occurring. This responsibility rests with management.

This is not too difficult a task if the nature of the business is 'potentially hazardous', for example coal mining, oil or gas production. However, it should be borne in mind that another type of crisis can arise — a financial one. Adverse publicity relating to a company's product or performance can have a devastating effect on the financial status of the company as current communications techniques will rapidly disseminate such information to all major markets. Last minute attempts to salvage a reputation may prove futile. The necessary work has to be done beforehand, in readiness for such an eventuality.

How can this be done?

The formulation of crisis management procedures is vital. Following an in-depth assessment of what might go wrong within your organization, it is then necessary to look at every potential problem area and attempt to come up with a solution.

I will address each topic in general terms as I think it is impossible to provide an overall set response to cover every company's potential problems. Generally speaking, however, there are three main response areas. These are operations, relative response and media response.

Operations

Management and senior personnel must be able to get on with the major task of coping with the crisis from an operational point of view. This may involve technical skills, for example, engineering, drilling and safety matters. On the other hand, it may involve corporate issues and product sales, or attempts to restore financial stability within the organization and confidence within national and international institutions and markets.

Whatever the main issues are, the fact remains that senior management must be in a position to cope with the overall

[67]

effects created by the crisis. In order that they can do this, support in other areas is absolutely vital.

Relative response

In the event that the crisis involves casualties or fatalities, the response from families, friends and the general public will probably be immense. An inability to cope effectively with this aspect will result in adverse publicity, extremely distressed staff and relatives and possibly the complete destruction of your company's image as a caring and responsible employer.

Media Response

Whether the crisis is of an operational nature involving financial loss, product failure which does not involve casualties/fatalities or a disaster which has resulted in casualties and loss of life, the one thing that can be guaranteed is that the media will want to know what happened and why it happened.

Should the organization involved not be able to respond promptly and effectively by providing as much information as possible to the media, then the consequences will be dire.

The influence of the press, TV and radio is immense. Given accurate, up-to-date information, they can be used as a means of informing millions of people of the facts. However, should any organization fail to provide such details, the media will undoubtedly seek information elsewhere and the inaccurate, speculative results may be very difficult, if not impossible, to overcome.

PROCEDURES

As I mentioned earlier, crisis management procedures should be compiled. These should contain a detailed description of what ought to be done and by whom, in the event of a crisis occurring.

Having identified the potential crises, action plans should be written for every scenario, clearly identifying the course of action to be taken.

Personnel likely to be involved should be briefed regarding their role in a crisis and any necessary training should be given. Staff must be familiar with these procedures in order that they can be implemented efficiently.

When a crisis occurs, trained competent staff are needed. 'Spare bodies' are of no use — they will only impede the efficiency of others.

PHYSICAL REQUIREMENTS

Operations control centre

Allocate space which can be set up as crisis centres. The nature of your business will dictate the equipment required in these rooms, but do ensure that there are sufficient telephone lines, fax machines and stationery items.

Log sheets

It is essential to maintain an ongoing record of events as they occur during an emergency situation. Log sheets should be completed by all operational personnel in the operations control centre. Not only do they provide an accurate record of events as they occur but they may be required as evidence in any subsequent inquiry into an incident.

Relative response centre

It is usually advisable to handle relative response from the personnel department location. Personnel files, next-of-kin information and other staff information can be accessed more easily by so doing.

Relative response is undoubtedly the most sensitive area and staff will usually be under some emotional stress while trying to cope with calls from distressed relatives, friends and colleagues. This should be borne in mind when considering staff working hours. Adequate communication equipment is again required and log sheets should be completed by all personnel involved in telephone response.

Other agencies

Should an emergency occur involving numerous casualties and/or fatalities, it will be necessary for your company personnel to work with representatives from the social services, hospitals and churches, as well as to assist families with travel plans, financial matters and accommodation. Such assistance may well involve personnel and their families from overseas.

Contractors

It is advisable to liaise closely with contractor companies, wherever they may be located, and if possible provide assistance as required. Small companies may not have adequate internal resources during a crisis and do often turn to the main company concerned for advice and assistance.

Media

Press calls will be received in the relative response centre and copies of all press releases should be passed to this location immediately upon release by the company. Care should be exercised when imparting the contents to the public. Usually, they are not concerned with hard facts but only with what has happened to their loved ones. However, there are exceptions when a journalist may simply wish to confirm a small detail, in which case the call can usually be handled by the relative response staff.

PRESS RESPONSE CENTRE

A room should be designated, in advance of any crisis, as a press room. Telephone lines should be installed and stationery, press packs and any other necessary equipment should be stored in a locked cupboard at that location, ready to be activated at very short notice.

A fax machine located in or near the press room is essential due to the large volume of written material required during an emergency which may have to be sent to locations worldwide.

Log sheets

Again, brief note pads recording callers names, publication and nature of enquiry are sufficient for use by press response staff. Time does not permit completion of a lengthier log.

Press room co-ordinator

A press room co-ordinator should always be present to whom difficult callers can be transferred. Close liaison must also be maintained with the operations and personnel departments to ensure that press releases contain accurate, up-to-date information. The co-ordinator should be responsible for the operation of the press room and ensure that staff are not being placed under too much pressure.

Technical advisers

Specialist information is often required by the press response co-ordinator. Such expertise should be made readily available during a crisis.

Internal communications

One area of crisis response which is often overlooked is that of internal communications. When an organization has several locations UK and worldwide, information relating to the crisis should be communicated to these locations as appropriate.

Do ensure that press releases are transmitted immediately from the main crisis centre to other locations where staff are attempting to respond to media/public enquiries.

E-mail

Efficient internal communications will enable all company locations to issue the same information simultaneously.

Consistent

STAFF TRAINING

There is little point in having emergency procedures, if you do not have staff who are capable of implementing them efficiently.

Press response team

It is most unusual for any company to have a large number of public relations staff. Many have none at all. Therefore, I recommend choosing a pool of staff from other departments. Personnel should be trained in dealing with press calls and should also familiarize themselves with the company's operations generally.

Relative response team

Due to the wide range of tasks which may have to be undertaken by the personnel department staff during a crisis, additional help may be required. Choose staff from other departments and train them accordingly. Ensure that they are also familiar with the company and its operation.

Company spokespeople

Who?

Official spokespeople should be appointed and the role identified in the crisis management procedures. Choose the person who will ultimately be identified as the 'company face' very carefully. The managing director is not always the best person for this job. Identify suitable personalities at all locations likely to be involved in a crisis and train these people in media relations. It is also invaluable for company spokespeople to receive television training.

Facing TV cameras and an interviewer can be a daunting task. But again, I would emphasize — do not wait until a real crisis occurs in order to test your capabilities.

[72]

There is no immediate short cut to achieving effective crisis management. Time, effort and money are all required. However, sound procedures implemented by well-trained personnel will enable your company to cope with a crisis.

In summary, I would recommend the following points for consideration. More precise requirements will of course depend upon the nature and size of your business.

- Prepare written procedures, identifying potential problems and specifying the course of action to be taken by management and staff.

- Ensure that your staff are familiar with these procedures by training them accordingly.

- Allocate specific duties to staff and again arrange appropriate training.

- Back-up staff should also be trained if possible, thereby ensuring that a complete crisis team is always available.

- Appoint official spokespeople and train these individuals in press handling.

- Conduct refresher sessions to ensure that new employees also become familiar with your procedures.

- Ensure that you have the physical capabilities to cope with a crisis. This may involve allocating space which can be converted at short notice into press/operations centres. Install the necessary communications equipment eg fax, telex, telephones.

- Prepare written background information on your company and its operation and make certain that your crisis team is familiar with such information. This material is also useful for distributing to the press.

- Senior management and your press spokespeople should receive television training. The thought of facing an interviewer and television cameras is rather frightening for the vast majority of people and TV training is decidedly beneficial. You do have a say in how an interview is conducted.

[73]

(PR Review)
question
(

- Lastly, but perhaps most importantly, endeavour to test procedures by running exercises based on a simulated crisis scenario. This will enable you to test not only the effectiveness of your procedures but will also enable your staff to practice their skills and become more familiar with new and probably very unfamiliar roles.

PIPER ALPHA

When I joined Occidental in May 1975, the structure known as the Piper jacket was being built and Piper Alpha came on stream in December 1976. No one with the company at that exciting time would ever have imagined that less than twelve years later, 167 men would tragically lose their lives when a series of explosions and fires destroyed the platform. Having already resigned from the company, my departure was delayed by several weeks. During that time, the world's attention was focused on the North Sea.

Many oil companies had already devoted considerable time and effort to crisis management. Since 1988, however, the North Sea oil industry has had to become even more aware of this aspect.

On 6 July 1988, as soon as the emergency was declared, Occidental's procedures were implemented. It was just after 10 pm when a telephone call from a local journalist asked if something had happened on board Piper Alpha. Having heard nothing, I said I would check. The telex room was manned 24 hours a day and our emergency call-out was handled by that staff. I was informed that the emergency call-out had been instigated.

I was able to drive to Occidental to arrive at approximately 10.15 pm. The telex operators continued the major emergency call-out which included most of the departments within operational headquarters in Aberdeen. At the same time, members of this emergency team informed relevant personnel at other locations, eg the London office. Within a short period of time, the full emergency team had assembled at the Bridge of Don offices.

For years, Occidental had devoted time and effort to establishing comprehensive emergency procedures. We had full management support and were consulted regarding our views relating to our specific areas. There had been a few emergencies in the past and exercises had been conducted to test the procedures. Video film of the exercises enabled us to examine the efficiency of the procedures, our response and to make any necessary changes.

Occidental had been the 'guinea pig' in a Norox Exercise, a full-scale emergency exercise run annually by the industry and associated authorities and organizations. By 1988, the company had well-formulated procedures, which had been put into practice in real and simulated emergency situations. Personnel were familiar with their roles.

I have referred to the three main areas of emergency response — operations, personnel response and media response. Within Occidental, those responsible for the individual areas had established teams of personnel familiar with their roles; training had been given and refresher training also, to ensure personnel did not forget or become complacent.

Responsibility lay with the head of every area so I took care of the press response team; the manager of human resources was responsible for the relative response team and all other personnel aspects. The vice-president of offshore operations was in charge of the operations control centre and its staff. The head of operations in Aberdeen was overall coordinator for the onshore emergency response.

In addition to an Emergency Procedures Manual, a 'quick guide', containing all relevant names and telephone numbers had been issued to the emergency team for retention at home. This enabled phone call contact to be made almost immediately after the initial call-out. Contact names and numbers of all authorities, eg Department of Energy, Department of Transport, Nature Conservancy Council, police, fire service, doctors, ambulance service and many more were listed in this

[75]

quick guide. In addition, all types of emergencies and their action plans were itemized.

What response facilities were available?

Space was at a premium. A fairly large training room on the second floor was used as the press response centre, and the main conference room, directly above, became the operations control centre. In order for these to be effective, additional equipment was, of course, required. Direct line telephones were installed which were activated only in an emergency situation. All stationery requirements were retained in locked cupboards, easily accessed when needed.

The 24-hour security and telex service not only alerted personnel but security staff also secured the building leaving only the main entrance as an access point. Staff were registered upon arrival and a personnel board indicated who had arrived and in which department/location they were. The staff restaurant and kitchens were opened up and remained operational 24 hours a day. During the first week, all personnel were fed, free, around the clock. Following the initial call-out, practical requirements were handled by the general services department.

How was 24-hour cover effected?

Press response centre

As mentioned earlier, all three main areas had someone in charge. Therefore, as part of the procedures, 'pools' of personnel were available for emergency duties. I had 30–35 staff (mainly administration/secretarial) drawn from various departments, who had been trained to respond to press calls.

As soon as the emergency was declared, the first eight members of staff were called out and a further eight called out and put on standby. There were eight incoming lines with other lines for my use. Staff living closest to the office were top of the call-out list. The back-up group was required should someone become upset because she had to deal with a distressing call or felt unable to continue for whatever reason. She would always be relieved immediately but this was seldom necessary. Besides it being unfair for anyone to work in such circumstances, the individual might say something completely wrong to a journalist.

The team usually settled down after about 45 minutes, the back-up team could be sent home to await a return call and a work schedule was soon established. All the team was female (except for technical advisers) and worked 4–5 hour shifts during the early days.

Relative response centre

The call-out was the same for all departments. The human resources department soon had its team assembled. They too had dedicated emergency lines as well as their extensions linked to the main switchboard number. Four lines were wholly dedicated to relatives' calls and these numbers were issued nationwide as soon as possible.

Relative response is undoubtedly the most stressful part of an emergency operation and the entire resources of this department were utilized. It had been recognized that additional help would be needed and extra staff from other departments had been trained for this task. During the disaster, retired personnel, other operators' personnel, and several staff wives were called in to help, such was the volume of work to be undertaken.

Police officers were located in this department for some time. They had lines allocated for their use. Constant contact had to be maintained with countless people and organizations.

Operations control centre

The practice in this centre was for those directly involved to be located in this room or staff worked from their own offices. If a drilling incident had occurred, it would have been likely that the drilling manager would have been located here along with all other support needed. However, the scale of this disaster meant that senior personnel from most of the technical departments spent much of their time in this centre. A model of the installation was brought in and TV/video equipment.

The senior manager in Aberdeen was also located here. He remained apart from the main group who were liaising with offshore operations regarding the search and rescue operation. His task was to coordinate all information from the entire emergency team and pass it to Occidental's management at other locations, other members of the consortium, government departments and other organizations.

Quick media interest

The media response was immediate. Having been alerted to the disaster by local press, I found out later that a news flash appeared on television shortly after 10 pm. Grampian TV covered the story throughout the night. On my arrival in the press room at approximately 10.15 pm, every line was buzzing.

The pressure and coping

There is no record of how many calls were received during the first few days. There were thousands and thousands of press calls from all over the world. Eight staff answered calls on a non-stop basis 24 hours a day. If the average length of call could be estimated as between 3 and 8 minutes, one can do the calculations.

Add to this the endless list of callers wishing to speak personally, eg Department of Energy Press Office, Police Scottish Office, Energy Minister's Office, the public relations colleague in London — Alex Blake-Milton, various Occidental people worldwide, local MPs, families of the deceased and literally dozens of people calling to express regret and offer words of comfort to families and Occidental staff — then one can imagine what it was like in the press room.

A major problem was only being able to be in one place at a time. The Press doorstepped our offices around the clock. On occasions, 20–40 reporters would attempt to get into the office. That usually brought a call from security asking for help. The journalists were generally seeking the latest news via an interview. Weeks afterwards, I realized these 'doorstep' interviews were being transmitted all over the country and abroad.

With my name often used, many callers would ask for me even if they did not know me. Quite a few relatives' calls came through. Whenever possible, I dealt with them — it would be impersonal to ask a distressed or concerned person to hang up and call again asking for the personnel department.

How did everyone cope? Because the occasion demanded that we had to and, to be fair, we had all received training and practice beforehand.

How often were press releases issued?

An emergency file was retained which contained a holding statement with a few blank spaces into which could be typed the installation name, date and time and press room contact number. This meant the initial statement could be completed in a matter of minutes and issued promptly. The holding statement, coupled with basic operational details on the company, gave the journalists something with which to work. Thereafter, press releases were issued when more information became available. As usual, the verification of details could take time and delay the issue of some statements.

During the early hours of 7 July, virtually no information was available and only scant details later in the day. Local journalists waited all night in the staff restaurant. At around 3 am we were all becoming aware that something terrible had happened.

As we succeeded in issuing press releases regularly, these went immediately to the London office, the police and the coastguard. The list of recipients grew as the days went by, including newspapers and publications worldwide.

The first press conference

Minister of Energy, Peter Morrison, flew to Aberdeen on 7

July. His first press conference was scheduled for approximately 8 am. Occidental's London-based chairman, John Brading, was also present. There were approximately 30 press representatives present and their camera equipment etc took up quite a lot of space which presented a problem.

After having flown offshore, the Minister gave a second conference attended by approximately 70 press representatives. The space in the staff restaurant was limited and as numbers were bound to increase, the site was changed to a large, nearby sports hall. Acoustics in such places are usually diabolical but it gave the needed commodity — space.

Dr Hammer and the Prime Minister flew in on the following day. Dr Hammer went to the hospital, coastguard headquarters and then met the Prime Minister at the offices. The members of the Press were like bloodhounds, seeking him out, following him everywhere. Mrs Thatcher left and then a press conference was held.

In excess of 150 journalists and photographers were present with lights, microphones and cameras. Already such issues as compensation, insurance costs, etc were being raised. Those present represented publications and television from all over the world. Their knowledge of the industry was varied. Some questions were probing but good, while others were positively ludicrous.

Thereafter, press conferences were held daily at, after consultation, 2 pm. John Brading faced the Press day after day. He succeeded in answering all questions. Red herrings and other issues emerged almost daily — A fire was seen earlier. A former employee says this or that. Were not drugs a problem offshore? Why was no report issued on a previous explosion? Is there a danger from chemicals? Why can divers not go down to recover the missing men? Will the food chain be affected? All questions had to be answered and at times several departments would be finding out operational details and facts which could be put into subsequent press releases.

The saddest part of the work was giving out details of casualties, known fatalities and those who remained missing. Careful checks had to be made before any information could be given out and this necessitated working very closely with the police. There was an Occidental representative based at the police headquarters incident room with whom we could liaise.

Photographs, video footage and diagrams depicting what was happening offshore were issued at the conferences and on most occasions there were 2–3 hours of answering further questions or getting more information. There were so many different things going on that it is virtually impossible to describe them all.

Red Adair was called in to assist and everyone wanted to interview him almost as soon as he had arrived. Questions started about how much he was being paid. Even if I had known, I would not have revealed the sum. Requests for him to appear on television were numerous. The *Wogan* show wanted to fly him down to London, have him appear and then return him. Such requests made one wonder if those involved in such programmes had any idea as to how serious the situation was offshore.

Every photographer wanted a photograph which was 'just a bit different'. It is best to issue the same to everyone. Showing favouritism causes huge problems for yourself and your company. No special material was issued to anyone. However, every endeavour was made to cooperate, such as a ship-to-shore contact between the Press Association and Red Adair on the basis that the Association reporter made the transcript available to anyone wishing to use it. This worked well.

A series of photographs, taken by men onboard an offshore vessel and the MSV Tharos, showed what had happened that night. They were subsequently confiscated by the police as evidence. An offer of a huge sum of money for a set of these was, needless to say, not accepted.

A few journalists indicated they would go any lengths to get 'that something extra' and there were times when one questioned whether some of them were actually human beings. However, more than 90 per cent of all the media representatives dealt with were reasonable. A few were quite

kind and considerate but they still wanted to know the facts —
that is the nature of their job.

Numerous people from all over the world called the press
room to say they knew how to solve the problem offshore.
Some were genuine, others were cranks. Suggestions on how
to extinguish the fires were forthcoming. Two men thought
they knew more than Red Adair and others said they had
solutions, but how much was Occidental prepared to pay? All
suggestions were passed on to a member of the technical staff.
After all, there might have been something valid in even one
idea but it was not a surprise when they all proved to be
useless.

Public response was extremely diverse. Many people hated
Occidental and anyone associated with the company or the oil
industry in general. Others were kind, writing moving letters
of comfort and support. School children sent prayers for the
men and their families. Indeed, the vast majority of people
were shocked and genuinely concerned for everyone
involved.

Professional counselling was made available to staff who felt
in need of help. Work with the families or the bereaved,
survivors, social services, different religious denominations,
the oil industry chaplain, and countless other groups continued for many months. In some cases, contact is still being
maintained and will continue as long as support is needed.

What happens to a company after a disaster?

Life must go on — this is often said and it is true. No one
involved will ever forget the men on Piper Alpha or what
happened on 6 July 1988. However, the fact remains that the
energy industry will always be pioneering. There will be many
new developments in the North Sea and elsewhere in the
world. We just hope and pray that there will never be another
disaster like Piper Alpha.

[82]

Lobbying Around the World

RICHARD LINNING

Richard Linning DipCAM, MIPR *is a consultant partner with Public Relations Partners in Brussels. He has previously worked in Australia, Hong Kong and the UK.*

The lessons learnt in these vastly different societies are now being applied to lobbying in the twelve member countries of the EC which, although contiguous, are in many respects as far apart as the countries of his earlier experience.

Is international lobbying a question of application of a standard set of principles or are there a new set of rules for each situation? In his opinion there is no easy answer.

CHAPTER FIVE

Lobbying Around the World

The most important thing in communication is to hear what isn't being said.

Peter F Drucker (1989) A World of Ideas —
Bill Moyers, *Doubleday*.

The activity which the word 'lobbying' describes is fundamental to the operation of a pluralist society. It is nothing more nor less than the free communication of a point of view and the public and private promotion of this opinion. There is no secret to lobbying: nor any guarantee of success.

In a free society, there are competing and often conflicting points of view on any issue. At all levels in such a society, there are mechanisms to resolve this competition of ideas, whether it is simply that father will have the final say in the family unit or that there will be a secret ballot in a parliamentary democracy. At its simplest then, any organized lobby activity probably has as its objective the persuasion of the decision-maker on the merits of a particular point of view.

Lobbying in this broad definition is a function of public relations, given the definition of public relations practice as 'the planned and sustained effort to establish and maintain goodwill and mutual understanding between an organization and its publics'. A lobbyist generally has the same objectives.

[85]

However, lobbying is often more specific. What is generally meant is political lobbying. Political lobbying is action exerted on the public authorities by individuals, whether in isolation or more generally by pressure groups, with the goal of defending their particular interests.

In the US, the combination of the scale of operation and past scandals and abuses, has led to the regulation of lobbying activity. Both legislators and lobbyists are required to observe strict — and legally enforceable — rules which inhibit, to an extent, the free communication and competition of opinion. But there are rules of acceptable behaviour in all democracies, spoken or unspoken, which are clearly marked and recognized features on the playing field on which ideas and lobbyists compete.

Deafness is an affliction frequently associated with cultural interfaces. The last stop on the railway linking the Atlantic and Pacific Oceans across Europe and Asia once stood on the harbour's edge in the British Crown Colony of Hong Kong. Vocal British expatriates protested loudly against its proposed demolition, citing in justification its historic importance in a colony founded in 1842. English-language newspapers and airwaves were flooded with letters and calls. Frustration, in the face of official indifference, turned to anger when the Chinese majority failed to support them. The paradox was that the blind certainty of their being right, in charges of cultural Philistinism by the lobbyists, left them unaware of the essential fact that, to the Chinese, this was an outdated example of British hegemony. The result — loss of face and destruction of a relic of the British Empire.

The pursuit of the goal of defending self-interest has given rise to two streams of activity which have been identified as 'pseudo lobbying' and 'pure lobbying'. Pseudo lobbying encompasses activities on the part of or by pressure groups soliciting public authorities to obtain from them favourable interpretations of laws and regulations, shorter intervention deadlines, or advantages deriving from administrative decisions. By contrast, 'pure lobbying' is or should have the

medium-term or long-term perspective of creating a favourable framework for the activity concerned. Public relations by
another name?

Within either perspective, goals and strategies must be
clearly defined and tactics of implementation focused. But, as
a letter published in *PR WEEK* (the UK trade paper)
demonstrates, this does not ensure success.

POLITICAL WINNER IS A 'LOSER'
Sometimes, I despair of the public relations industry's understanding of the complex world of politics.

The news that Paragon Communications has won the award
for the best political campaign in the *PR WEEK* awards only
serves to confirm my pessimism.

I had the privilege of being inside the Department of Trade
and Industry as special adviser to Lord Young while Paragon
was waging its campaign on behalf of the brewers and against
the Monopolies and Mergers Commission Report. Although
aspects of the brewers' campaign were brilliant, notably the
mobilization of the small and regional brewers to attack a
report intended to help them and the resultant parliamentary
support for the brewers' case, I feel much of Paragon's work
was counter-productive.

In particular, the advertising campaign launched, according
to your 'citation' on the advice of Paragon, nearly destroyed
any chance of rational debate. Advertising intended to change
the minds of ministers is only rarely appropriate: at best it is
likely to be a waste of money; at worst, as in this case, it will
make it impossible for ministers to change any aspect of their
declared intentions since, by heightening the confrontation,
even modest amendments will inevitably be interpreted as a
climbdown.

On this occasion, the advertising was more than usually
damaging to the brewers. Before it appeared, 90 per cent of
the letters received by the DTI were stimulated by the brewers
and attacked the MMC Report. The campaign, by drawing the
general public's attention to the issue, transformed this dramatically and the balance changed to 80 per cent of letters
supporting the report. For the first time, the DTI had evidence
of massive public support for the proposed changes.

[87]

What was even worse was that the pubs it showed were alleged to be threatened with closure yet were all highly profitable, as a number of national newspapers and an edition of *This Week* disclosed.

Finally, it is worth remembering that the campaign failed. The judges fell for Paragon's claim that 'the final outcome was a backdown by the Government which virtually assured a retention of the status quo'. Try telling that to the brewers.

The most recent report I have seen on the subject — in *Property Week* — said Lord Young has 'set in motion a chain of events that will almost certainly herald the break-up of the tied system and the start of a potentially ugly pricing war between the brewers'. Some status quo.

Peter Luff, London SE3

Even if a simple set of guidelines for lobbying can be stated, such as identifying the decision-makers, their advisers and those whose unsolicited advice may be favourably received, there is no guarantee, in a free society, of how the argumentation will be received. Indeed, the result may be counter-productive.

It is not often that 'insiders' are as free in their critical assessment of the effects of a lobbying campaign as was Peter Luff. From his privileged position within the Department of Trade (the decision-maker), he was able to observe the impact on civil servants (advisers) of the campaign (unsolicited advice).

Another example from the private sector — companies can be lobby targets too — was published in *The Economist*. Here, the sports shoe manufacturer Nike was the target of a campaign for increased contracts and jobs for blacks — a major market for them. As the item indicates, the organizers clearly misjudged public (black) support. Another case of not hearing what was being said.

WHEN SHOVE CAME TO PUSH
There is an assumption that political lobbying is the pejorative preserve of the giants of commerce and industry. But they may also be the target.

[88]

The plan seemed simple enough. Operation PUSH would demand that Nike, an athletic-shoe behemoth, hand out contracts and jobs for blacks in proportion to the amount of business blacks gave Nike, which is a lot. If Nike did not cooperate, PUSH — founded by Jesse Jackson in the 1960s — would roll up the heavy artillery: a boycott of Nike products.

PUSH demanded. Nike parried. PUSH boycotted. Result: Nike's best quarter ever and forward orders that surpass projections.

A noisy rally by PUSH at Nike's shareholders' meeting gave the whole endeavour the look of crude thuggery. And a Gallup poll in Chicago, where PUSH has its headquarters, shows that people support Nike by 3:1.

PUSH seems to have badly misjudged its ability to rally blacks to its cause. Its hope was to wean urban youth from the flashy, pricey athletic shoes that have become the inner-city equivalent of the pin-striped suit on Wall Street. Despite extensive media coverage of the boycott and the demonstrations outside shoe shops, PUSH seems to have won few converts. One Chicago shop even reported customers buying Nike shoes in protest against the PUSH boycott.

And questions are being raised about the boycott's stated goal. Nike's domestic employment is almost entirely devoted to marketing development and financial matters: the shoes themselves are made overseas.

(The Economist, *22 September 1990.*)

THE ROLE OF RESEARCH

Drucker's comment about hearing what is not being said is particularly appropriate to the conduct of a successful lobby. Research is an indispensable aid to 'hearing'. The combination of factors which together produce a 'decision' are many. The worth of a particular case alone is insufficient. Remember that it was the willingness of the real mother to give up her child which persuaded Solomon, in his wisdom, of the truth of her claim. Research is essential to understand the process of decision-making. (That of the EC is discussed in detail later.)

Understanding the process identifies the opportunities for intervention, for putting a point of view. Ongoing research can be called intelligence gathering; knowing precisely where the issue is 'at', what information the decision-makers have, what they lack, who else is taking an interest. Armed with this information, a lobbyist is in a position to be proactive: he can gain the advantage of the high ground. An example of this is the aluminium can recovery campaign in Italy, quoted later.

There is a further advantage. Given this information, an organization may alter its objective, message or target(s) in order to more effectively pursue its aims. It is also given time to consider what it can concede. In politics, an objective should always be satisfaction for both parties, not winning or losing. Losers will always try to get even.

LESSONS WITH UNIVERSAL APPLICATION

Whether it is domestic or international lobbying, the key elements remain. Objective definition, message and means. What is always different is the target audience. In the multi-racial societies of the world's biggest cities, the audiences can be as cross-cultural as any international one. How best to communicate? What media have credibility is a question which you have to ask for each street, town, country — for any audience.

In 'International media relations' in *Public Relations Quarterly* (Summer 1989, New York), John M. Reed set the question in Latin America:

> To have an impact in Panama on the political and business elite, what is the optimum choice? The choice is from three TV channels, several radio stations, newspapers in English for the whole community, English for the black community and Spanish for the rest of the community.

> The correct answer? None of the above. The ideal outlet is a monthly newsletter of the Golf and Country Club. Anyone who is anyone belongs to the Golf and Country Club and carefully reads the newsletter.

The elected member of parliament — any parliament — is the archetypal lobbyist. On the one hand, he has his policy objective; on the other, his reading of opinion that is in support for the issue — or, to put it another way, the direction the wind is blowing. The measure of his political skill is in setting his sails and course to reach his objective, or, alternatively, in choosing the equally acceptable but achievable compromise destination.

The first lesson a politician or a lobbyist has to learn is that he will not always get everything his own way in the democratic process. A US energy company, Associated Octel, which puts lead into petrol, conducted a failed lobbying campaign in the EC which is now the much-quoted example of what not to do.

The company threw a spectacular — over-ostentatious — party to try to influence the views of members of the European Parliament (MEPs) on a plan for cutting lead in petrol. It succeeded only in encouraging them to go for even lower lead levels than had been proposed. 'We gave them a pretty rough evening' Ken Collins MEP, chair of the European Parliament's Environment Committee at the time, recalls.

The second lesson is that it is easier to sail with the wind. Decision-taking in the EC, as elsewhere, is a long, drawn-out process. It is the conclusion of investigation and discussion; examination of competing arguments; compromise. Long before the decision is taken, a broad consensus emerges. The momentum of opinion tending in this one direction makes the conclusion almost inevitable. Once the institutional momentum has developed, it is hard to stop.

Certainly in Europe, it is grossly misleading to suggest, as many Americans believe of their own legislative process, that there exists a 'silver bullet' — someone of overwhelming power and influence — who can stop the rolling snowball of opinion in its tracks. The deficit at the centre of the EC is not one of democracy but one of power. It is the same almost everywhere. To lobby in Europe is not a matter of proposing or opposing but of participation.

[91]

The third lesson then is that the decision-making process is one of continuous dialogue. In the EC, for example, to the outsider, the amount of dialogue between conception of a proposal and publication of the final decision in the Official Journal (OJ) may not be immediately obvious. A moment's reflection, however, will give some clue as to the number of participants.

The Commission's decisions are collegiate so that at least 17 Commissioners, their cabinets and 23 Directorates General (DGs) are involved. Then there are twelve Member States, with a permanent representative, technical expert and so on each, plus the 518 members of the European Parliament to varying degrees, the EP's administrators and political group staffs — and, of course, the lobbyists outside the institutions, industry and consumers . . . and so on. The number is large!

LISTENING IS AN ART

The word dialogue is often misunderstood. It is more than a conversation. It is an 'exchange' of opinions. It is both speaking and listening. A good listener is a good lobbyist.

Lobbying is part monitoring, part intervention. Intelligence should produce not just copies of documents but a feel for political intentions and temperature, context and intuition — the foundation for successful intervention.

The most profitable role for a lobbyist can be one of coalition building, for sometimes the strangest of bedfellows have the most to gain from joining forces. Often it takes an outsider to point it out. Not infrequently he is also the best informed.

The most successful lobbyist in Thailand is Mechai Viravaidya. Ask for Mechai in Bangkok and you will be handed a condom, for his name is now synonymous with the product the use of which he has promoted since 1974. So successful has he been that the World Bank gives him credit for 'one of the most successful and effective family planning programmes in the world'. The Mechai method works in

Thailand — and can be applied elsewhere — because it is about participation in the art of communication. Condom-blowing competitions in schools, bars and shops have bred a familiarity with the subject and so succeeded in demystifying birth control. If people laugh, they are more likely to be on your side: that is his simple and successful philosophy. He might have added, and more likely to be receptive to your message.

DECEPTIVELY SIMPLE

The Treaty of Rome which is shaping post-1992 Europe was likened by Lord Denning, the UK legal sage, to 'an incoming tide'. He observed 'it flows into estuaries and up the rivers. It cannot be held back.' As a consequence for individuals, organizations and countries, the process of reshaping Europe cannot be ignored by anyone. This explains why Brussels now has probably the largest concentration of lobbyists in the world.

Regulation, directive and recommendation are the three forms of EC legislation. The process of drafting and implement-ing them can appear deceptively simple. The Commission prepares the initial draft and the Council of Ministers decides the final version but only after consulting both the European Parliament and the Economic and Social Committee. National governments are responsible for implementation. The other principal EC institution, the Court of Justice, adjudicates on disputes.

Simple, but not quite so simple. Each instrument is dis-tinctly different. A regulation is binding on all Member governments and requires no national legislation; a directive must be incorporated into national law; and a recommenda-tion is no more than that — a non-binding Community view of a topic.

Draft to decision

The drafting is not straightforward either. A draft proposal is

[93]

normally prepared by the permanent staff of the Commission in one of the Directorates General with responsibility for a specific policy area, agriculture for example. This is not formally proposed to the Council of Ministers until the Commission, collegiately, has approved the draft and the legal base for it. The legal base determines the decision-making route that the proposed legislation will take.

So, the process of drafting and implementation is both a simple and a complex procedure. But, significantly for lobbyists, it is also open and evolving. Open yes, but the welcome for a lobbyist will be greater if contact at each level is appropriate. Technical expert should talk to technical expert; managing director to department head; president of the company to commissioner or prime minister. It is a waste of resources to use a sledge hammer to crack a nut.

At all stages — in the initial drafting in the Commission; in the national considerations which contribute to determining the Council's common position; in the work of the European Parliament's committees and rapporteurs — it is possible to provide solicited or unsolicited input. In fact, if the input is factual and objective it is positively welcomed, even from lobbyists.

It is so open that there is a risk. As Professor Yves Meny, a French expert on EC legislation has warned, 'the Community's decision-making process carries within itself the seeds of bad application because good political compromises create bad policies'.

CONCLUSION

Is lobbying simply the rigid application of a set of principles? It would be misleading to think so. There is a broad methodology, nothing more. First find the answers to these questions:

• Who makes the decision?

• Who gives the advice on which decision will be made?

[94]

- Who can introduce more information which will be acceptable?

In other words, the currency of lobbying is information. The more that is known and understood about the situation and the people involved, the more chance there is of exerting an influence. So, if there is a guiding principle, it is this: use the ears before the mouth and, particularly, listen for what is not being said.

Example

The aluminium can recovery campaign in Italy, quoted earlier as an example of the use of research/intelligence gathering to achieve proactive lobbying, was carried out as follows.

Anticipating the possible introduction of compulsory collection and recycling legislation, an Italian market leader in the soft drink sector launched in 1986 a can recovery programme to demonstrate to the authorities the viability of a voluntary scheme and, in the event of a legal regime, the realistic recovery rates.

One billion aluminium cans were sold in Italy in 1985; none was recycled. The recycling figures for the US and Switzerland were 55 per cent and 77 per cent respectively, but in those countries collection and recycling are required by law.

The company had three aims: to reduce pollution and waste of resources; to contribute to the recovery of cans by influencing public opinion, the 'recoverers' and recyclers of waste material and public authorities; and, of equal importance, to prevent or head off potentially punitive legislation which might impose penalties on the cans themselves.

Clearly, the communication programme had to go hand in hand with the recovery of cans and the provision of suitably equipped foundries. The company involved decided not to get involved under its own name and a consortium of five international companies with interests in Italy was formed.

[95]

The target public

This may be divided into five parts:

- public opinion as a whole;

- those already engaged in the field — waste recoverers, local councillors who favour protection of the environment and collection/recovery of refuse, and legislators;

- the Press;

- local authorities;

- those sectors of the public most exposed to environmental and educational concerns — schools, voluntary associations and the like.

The test area was established. It was determined on the basis of the high per capita consumption of carbonated soft drinks from aluminium cans and on its strategic importance in terms of both politics and image. The choice fell on Milan.

Media response to the launch of the programme was positive. Schools provided the primary target for the collection of cans. The promotion in schools reached various voluntary organizations which cooperated with the consortium. In particular, in 1987, AIDO (The Italian Association of Human Organ Donors) built a 1:10 scale model of the Colosseum with 1,250,000 aluminium cans recovered throughout Italy. This project found its way into *The Guinness Book of Records* and received much media exposure — including foreign media. Other similar projects followed.

Local authorities join in

In the summer of 1987, the councils of Ravenna and Rimini became involved, taking in the seaside resorts along the whole of the country's Adriatic coastline. By the end of 1989, about 600 Italian councils were involved.

The first phase of the campaign highlighted the usefulness of recovering aluminium as a raw material. Subsequently, it stressed the protection of the environment through civic education and action. As a direct consequence, in 1987, a bill was introduced into the Italian Parliament to render the differential collection of refuse (including aluminium) obligatory for all Italian councils. This led to a law imposing differential collection of refuse on councils and the setting up of obligatory national consortia for recycling of raw materials.

Results

In 1986, 67 tons of aluminium cans were recycled; in 1987, 229 tons; in 1988, 657 tons; and in the first eight months of 1989, 2,000 tons — equal to about 10 per cent of the cans produced and sold in Italy in that year.

The campaign was confined to Italy but is now an example for other countries. At the end of 1989, an association of aluminium packaging producers and users was established to continue the campaign at European level.

[97]

Consumer Marketing Worldwide

ANN LINSCOTT

Ann Linscott JP, MIPR *began her career in an advertising agency, moving on to in-house experience in marketing, advertising and public relations. She was appointed director of public relations for Royal Doulton Ltd in 1974 and is now director of corporate communications, responsible for public relations, advertising, display, factory tours and museums. Her company is a world leader in the manufacture and distribution of fine china, employing some 8,000 people in UK factories, retail outlets and overseas distribution companies.*

Outside her job, she has served as a magistrate for 13 years and has held many official and consultative positions within social, business and charitable organizations.

Consumer Marketing Worldwide

The Gulf War of 1991 was a fascinating study for international public relations students, for here was a war where the ability of presidents and generals to communicate internationally through television and other media was an integral part of the military strategy. Generals had to be as much concerned with public opinion at home as with running the war. Keeping their public's belief in the justness of the cause; preparing them for the inevitable horrors of the loss of human life; recognizing that items designed for home consumption were being watched by the enemy in the bunker.

Future historians may see this war as the first to be fought through satellite television waves as much as traditional armoury. Just one year before the Gulf War, democracy had been allowed into Eastern Europe with the fall of communist regimes in such countries as Poland, Czechoslovakia and Eastern Germany. Many observers believe that it was the constant showing of Western living standards and the democratic process that made the demand for change so irresistible.

The dramatic growth and expansion of information technology during the past decade means that the public relations professional today operates in an international arena. Some may specialize in the home market, but all will need an appreciation of global activities to be truly successful. It is vital that, in the UK for instance, membership of the international, European and home country communities is accepted as the norm.

There are still companies which divide their marketing, promotional and selling activities between home and over-seas. In their recent book, *Managing Across Borders* (1989, Business Books Ltd), Christopher Bartlett of the Harvard Business School and Sumantra Ghosal of France's INSEAD Business School identified four types of 'world' company. The first they called simply 'global' and defined them as organizations still looking to a centralized headquarters for their strategic direction. 'International' companies are still heavily dependent on the parent firm, but more decentralized. Then, the 'multinational' companies which are highly decentralized, with each country subsidiary operating relatively autonomously, and, lastly, the 'transnational' company. This is the ideal, the company which thinks globally but acts locally as conditions dictate. A company with a worldwide vision unhindered by home-country prejudices.

For the businessman, a sound public relations programme may be even more essential abroad than at home. There are often patriotic preferences for home-produced goods over foreign brands; preferences which competitors will be sure to use to their advantage. Manufacturing abroad may also pose problems. For instance, the UK now, but perhaps in some cases reluctantly, accepts Japanese and German manufacturing but this is still not true of the rest of Europe. The foreign manufacturer may be feared not just for being different; there may be genuine concern about high wages attracting the best workers and doubts about the long-term commitment to a locality of the incoming enterprise.

Just as we work within the culture of our own country when planning public relations strategy, when operating on the international scene it is necessary to begin by understanding and appreciating the business and social structure of individual markets.

THE PUBLIC RELATIONS PROGRAMME

There are many questions which must be answered before deciding to organize an overseas public relations programme.
First — the environment:

- What is its balance between industrial and rural living?

- What is the family income?

- What is the political/legal situation?

- Is it politically stable?

- What are the monetary regulations?

- Most importantly — can one's money be got out?

- What of the government bureaucracy?

- How is the cultural environment?

- What about the business traditions?

Good groundwork and research will provide the answers — each one of which could be fundamental to the success of a campaign. An understanding of the culture is vital. For instance, in markets such as Japan it would be unwise to assume that business can be done without the assistance of a native individual or organization. There is just too much for a foreigner to learn and get wrong.

The first-time visitor to Japan would be well advised not to bow — because of the difficulty in getting it right. In Japan the bow is not a simple courtesy. The depth and style is dictated by the relevant status of the greeter and the greeted. In the exchange of business cards, which is essential in Japan, the card represents the person and therefore the treatment of the card and the length of time for which it is looked at reflect the respect held for the giver. Even the business meeting has a different structure and form to that in the West.

In Japan, a one-to-one meeting is virtually unknown. Decisions are taken at a relatively junior level of the hierarchy and approved all the way up to the company president. This means that representatives from each level need to attend meetings. The first meeting is likely to concentrate on pleasantries as the Japanese sensibly prefer to take time to get to know the people with whom they are considering working. However, once the decision to cooperate has been made, the project proceeds rapidly with cooperation at all levels.

Respecting the nuances of an ancient and honourable culture is essential and having the assistance of a colleague born into the culture is invaluable. In Japan, finding a colleague who can appreciate the Western culture enough to break the seemingly impenetrable politeness and so be able to tell you when you are wrong is absolutely wonderful. It is easy to see where mistakes can be made. Everyone has heard stories of the typical Englishman abroad who thinks that shouting somehow improves the understanding of foreign-speaking natives. In international public relations, we need to listen, learn and appreciate the people with whom we are working before adapting our strategy to achieve our goal.

LOCAL PUBLIC RELATIONS

Peter Biddlecombe, author of *Goodwill — the Wasted Asset* (1971, London Business Books), suggests that in assessing the potential for a locally based public relations operation overseas, it is necessary to consider the following:

1. Are the local Press and television willing to accept public relations news releases or do they expect payment?

2. What types of promotion are acceptable?

3. Can the local media accept tie-in promotions?

4. Does the government have a strong 'corrupt practices' branch? This can be very restricting.

5. What is the local attitude to sponsorship?

6. What of the vexed question of charity donations? They can be construed as bribes.

7. Can newspaper supplements be used? These can be very useful overseas.

8. Is there a local trade, technical or specialist press? Always the best core beginning for a public relations campaign.

9. Apart from market research, there must be a correctly drawn up public relations attitude survey.

10. Always remember that an organization's local standing can affect its credit rating — and who will work for it.

When satisfied that the market has the potential for a successful public relations campaign, the best agent available should be hired. Take care and time in the search — it will not be easy. In less-developed countries, good agents are few and far between. The commercial counsellor at the embassy and representatives of the companies already operating successfully in the market will be a source of contacts. Also, look at multinational consultancies which have set up offices abroad or established reciprocal agreements within a network of nationally based organizations.

Once the agent has been selected, spend time with them. Overseas public relations people need to meet home-based executives, and know them as individuals in order to encourage knowledge and involvement in the business. Team work, too, has to be international.

RESEARCH

Successful public relations is always research based and there are a multitude of attitudinal and motivational studies published each year on markets, trends and consumers. They are excellent to give background information before any specialist studies are commissioned. Missions organized by government or trade organizations are particularly useful to give a general introduction to a market or a specific sector.

For instance, a British Tourist Authority (BTA) mission, under government auspices, went out to Japan to see how the number of Japanese tourists to the UK could be increased. The visit was really a chance to gain first-hand information to back up extensive research on the social factors which influence the choice of destination. In fact, the research was of interest to anyone wanting to sell consumer goods or services in a market which is dominated by brand awareness. The 'Made in England' label, for instance, is important in the selling of such prestigious consumer goods as bone china.

It is always useful to know how other nations see us and the BTA research covering Japanese perceptions in key words was particularly revealing:

- *Spain*: cheerful — sunshine — underdeveloped — white houses — oily — dry — red soil — siesta

- *US*: affluence — freedom — wide area — subway — Times Square — fast food — AIDS — cowboys

- *France*: stubborn — fashionable — artistic — difficult language to learn — argumentative — romantic — Eiffel Tower — French chateaux

- *Germany*: beer — pork — BMW cars — autobahn — sausages — Hitler — hard-working

- *UK*: classy — obsolete — biased — silly — gentlemen — refined — barbarian — grey — Princess Diana — dark — black taxis — English breakfasts — pubs.

In overseas public relations the preconceived notions of the host country have to be taken into account when planning a campaign.

Another important consideration is language. Being able to communicate directly with an international audience is the ideal which is not usually practical. It shows commitment to learn just a few phrases for everyday use, but an expert translator should always be available. Ensure that important documents are translated from English and then back into English. Remember the Colgate case? A campaign was launched to promote a new toothpaste which came out of the tube like a ribbon and lay flat on the toothbrush. This was translated literally to read: 'Colgate viene ahora en cintra.' To the Latin-American, this meant: 'Colgate now comes pregnant.'

RESPONSIBILITY

Everyone has a different definition of public relations and its responsibility within an organization. Some 75 per cent of public relations functions within the UK are positioned in the marketing function, whereas there is general agreement that public relations is most effective when directly responsible to the chief executive. This close relationship with the chief executive becomes more important when dealing with international public relations because, unless responsibility is seen to be at the centre, the strains of split responsibility to host country and parent organization can create difficulties.

It is essential that sound policies are established. Where several countries are involved, a uniform policy is essential. Because of the complexities in dealing with public opinion in so many countries, with so many differences in language, politics, customs, motivations and internal pressures, the variety of public relations service required is virtually endless.

IN-HOUSE OPERATION

Many companies are reorganizing their public relations function so that they can assume a global role. Royal Doulton, which sells 50 per cent of its output overseas, has recently established a corporate communications department, responsible to the chief executive, which incorporates advertising, display and public relations. The aim is that the company should speak with one voice, whether in shop displays, promotions or public relations activities. It allows the people working in each of the specialist areas to use their particular expertise to achieve the company mission and to come

[107]

together in joint projects. For instance, a bridal promotion developed in the UK was advertising led, but with substantial public relations and display support. It has now been successfully introduced into the US and Canada, with local adaptations. A good simple concept can be adapted for successful international use, with the central team liaising with their colleagues in the overseas countries. Outside public relations consultants are chosen to work on specific projects as and when required.

NEWS

Most organizations like to generate news which draws attention to their virtues. The UK-based, standard news release will usually assume a considerable background either of topical news or of the common culture — which makes it inappropriate for overseas use. On the other hand, certain topics or events will attract overseas interest. Abroad, a Royal visit to an organization may stimulate greater interest than at home. Covering the right event in the UK with a company news story can be effective in achieving extensive overseas coverage. Royal Doulton, for example, gained worldwide television coverage by unveiling a clay model of Princess Diana within hours of the announcement of the Royal wedding.

Public relations also needs to be ready to deal with a crisis, when speaking with one informed voice may be crucial. The speedy worldwide response of Perrier to the adulteration of its product illustrates how crisis has to be met head on.

Both contrasting examples underline the need for very close cooperation and understanding between various sectors of the company and the press representatives in different parts of the world. A company or organization may not be large enough to have overseas press representation. In these circumstances, it is more important than ever to investigate and use the often underrated services of the Central Office of Information (COI), the government information service.

The COI has specialists covering all parts of the world who will advise on suitable media and circulate appropriate news stories and photographs; arrange visits by national or specialist sector journalists; and generally advise on overseas promotional activities. There as also news agencies, such as Reuters, which will distribute hard news stories, and a large core of overseas correspondents in both television and other media, based in London. Associate membership of the Foreign Press Association (FPA) is useful in establishing and building personal contacts.

EXHIBITIONS

Many of the UK's long-established and leading companies enhance their reputation by participating in exhibitions. In the Sir Henry Doulton Gallery in Burslem there are numerous gold medals from international fairs held in such cities as Chicago, Paris and Vienna. Having participated in the 1851 Great Exhibition at the Crystal Palace, Victorian businessmen grasped the opportunity to show off their skills at prestigious venues.

The power of the exhibition continues to expand in many countries, with some cities, such as Frankfurt, Birmingham, Milan, and many others, specializing in promoting large fairs. The importance of such exhibitions in product promotion can be judged by the international media coverage of the Geneva Car Show. However, at the same time, the growth of the international audience has meant an explosion in costs, so that only the largest companies can afford major representation. But, there are good value-for-money opportunities in niche (specialized) market exhibitions, many of them supported by UK government agencies such as the Department of Trade and Industry.

For promotion direct to the consumer, the sophisticated department stores in many of the major markets offer the opportunity to mount small quality exhibitions linked, if possible, with demonstrations of craftsmanship. Here, the space costs nothing and there is the tremendous advantage of being close to the point of sale.

GUIDELINES

To summarize, the world of business and commerce has, indeed, become a global village even for quite small organizations. International public relations is essential for almost every activity whether political, cultural or commercial. The guidelines for success are simple:

- Participate: take advantage of every opportunity to learn more about overseas markets.

- Research: fully research the market.

- Observe: visit the market to gain first-hand experience.

- Strategy: develop strong, central strategies capable of individual market adaptation and implementation.

- Partnership: choose with care the agent or individual representative with whom you will work.

- Enthuse: make your chosen international partners feel enthusiastic members of the organization.

- Respond: be capable of responding quickly to the demands of individual markets — in particular, coping with time differences.

It is no coincidence that the initial letters of these points form the word PROSPER. Ed Murrow, the US and international broadcaster and information director, once said 'It is what we do — more than what we say — that has the greatest impact overseas.'

The author would like to thank Herbert Lloyd BA, FRSA, DipCAM, FIPR for his help with advice and contribution in the preparation of this chapter. Herbert is a past-president of the IPR and a very experienced practitioner who has embodied his knowledge in a basic, practical book on public relations (*Public Relations* rev. ed. 1980, Hodder and Stoughton).

CHAPTER SEVEN

International Business-to-Business Public Relations

DAVID WATSON

David Watson MA, MIPR *graduated from St John's College, Cambridge, in 1972 with an honours degree majoring in philosophy. After a short period with the public relations subsidiary of a large advertising agency he joined Infopress in 1973.*

Working mainly with consumer and business-to-business clients, David first became involved in international work in 1974 when creating a pan-European visibility campaign for a major exhibition in the audio industry.

In 1984, he was appointed managing director of Infopress, one of the largest independent public relations consultancies in the UK with considerable experience of working across international boundaries.

Two years later, he took the firm into membership of PRX International, a corporation founded in 1983, the members of which are leading independently owned public relations companies with offices in over 60 cities worldwide, providing a comprehensive range of communication services. From November 1991, David is president of PRX International.

International Business-to-Business Public Relations

INTRODUCTION

In the UK in 1989, over 300 million international phone and fax calls were made through British Telecom International alone. Twenty-five years ago, the figure was only one-hundredth of this, and indeed it was not until 1963 that it was possible to direct-dial an international call from the UK — and that was London to Paris only. Contacts with the rest of the world have clearly expanded dramatically in the last few years and they continue to do so.

A significant proportion of this colossal volume of communication traffic is, needless to say, involved in conducting business and it is therefore not surprising that international business-to-business public relations is blossoming. Among public relations work carried out on the international front, it has perhaps the longest track record in the field: from the trade fairs and export drives of the 1950s and 1960s, through branch office support in the old 'Empire' territories to today's

scenario. Now there are global brands, international networking and easy cross-border communication driving the business world ever closer to the global village model.

Before looking in outline at some of the factors to bear in
mind when handling cross-border public relations work in the
business sector, it is perhaps worth stating that business-to-
business public relations in the UK refers to work carried out
in support of organizations the customers of which are other
businesses. There is clearly, within this sector, a huge variety
of subject matter — everything from speciality chemicals and
biotechnology through engineering, electronics and software
to financial, professional and management services.

A GROWING AND SIGNIFICANT MARKET

The general move towards the lowering of international trade
barriers (between the US and Canada, and within the EC for
example) coupled with the continuing work done by GATT
ensures a global trading environment positively disposed to
the conducting of business across national borders.

Expansion

When it comes into being at the beginning of 1993, the
European single market will contain 320 million people and
be 30 per cent larger than the US. The potential for cross-
borders sales and marketing in such an environment, and
consequently business-to-business public relations support, is
enormous.

When one adds to this the opportunities for commercial
access to Eastern Europe, greatly assisted by German unifica-
tion, scope for business-to-business firms to go to market
abroad becomes even greater. The gradual abandonment of
centrally planned markets, together with the opening up of
borders, means that countries previously considered together
as the Eastern bloc (Hungary, Poland, Czechoslovakia, etc)

now offer medium- to long-term scope as markets for business — and therefore for public relations professionals operating in this sector.

The market for cross-border public relations services has grown rapidly during the last five years, and vastly improved communication is partly responsible for this. European public relations companies made over 20 per cent of their fees in 1989 on international work (according to a survey entitled *The economic importance and future of public relations agencies in Europe*, published by the International Committee of Public Relations Consultancies Associations Members — ICO for short). Twelve months earlier, this figure was only 5.8 per cent.

Choice

While trade barriers have been gradually falling and new markets have been opening up, the amount of choice for the business purchaser has been increasing dramatically. The cost and ease of international travel, combined with the explosion in telecommunications and computer power has produced an international marketplace in which even small companies can sell their products and services abroad.

Niche marketing

The trend towards niche marketing (targeting relatively small, tightly defined audiences with specifically tailored product and service benefits) has assisted in this process, enabling smaller organizations to be significant players in global, but specialist, markets. Where previously only larger organizations could afford the infrastructure and time to investigate and participate in foreign markets, now even very small companies can realistically exploit opportunities more or less anywhere in the world.

Speed

The public relations professional should be aware of another critical element implicit in these changes. The ease with which it is possible to communicate internationally has speeded up the whole process. Telephone, fax, voice messaging and electronic mail (e-mail) cross borders at lightning speed; and the media (both print and broadcast) now transcend national boundaries more than ever before. Business-to-business media, reflecting the trend towards niche marketing, have been in the forefront of this development.

In addition, the massive proliferation of computer databases and information-gathering systems has made much more information available much more rapidly.

THE PUBLIC RELATIONS RESPONSE

In the business-to-business sector, a great variety of work is now carried out internationally — from defining and communicating issues and concepts (such as 'open systems' or 'clean exhaust gases') to straight product marketing support work. Public relations professionals have responded to the challenge in a variety of ways. Organizations using in-house departments have set up links with satellite offices in their foreign operations or with the public relations people deployed by distributors and agents. Public relations companies have used a range of approaches: setting up their own offices in key locations; acquiring 'local' public relations companies; and networking — either informally or through a more structured organization such as PRX International, WORLDCOM or Pinnacle. Whatever the approach, public relations practitioners in the business-to-business sector face common problems and opportunities.

Global public relations?

In fact, there are few global companies and brands in business-to-business marketing and such activity tends to be market specific and mainly confined to the 'industrialized' countries. Global public relations strategies are frankly rare, but they *can* be vital. When Infopress launched ICI's imaging and business graphics operation — ICI Imagedata — in early 1988, a strategy was developed which included targeting business partners in Japan and end users in the US and Europe, phased over a period of years. With different jobs to do in different countries, the overall marketing strategy entailed country-specific public relations approaches, and this is true of every successful 'global' strategy.

Public relations professionals need to remember that organizations which are well known in some parts of the world are not necessarily high profile in others. Samsung, Korea's largest company and the 20th largest company in the world, is much better known in Australasia than in the UK, for example, and public relations approaches need to take account of this. In addition, companies may position their brands and products differently according to local market conditions: a premium brand in an established marketplace may well need to be positioned as 'low cost, value for money' elsewhere in the world in order to establish a competitive foothold in that market. Failure to recognize and respond to this can lead to totally inappropriate public relations work.

Local conditions

The successful public relations professional, while learning from the experiences of the company or brand in its various markets, recognizes that what works in one country does not necessarily work in another: individual countries need individual strategies. Businesses buy in different ways in different countries. Distribution networks vary widely and different types of support are needed to cope with these variations.

In addition, countries themselves are organized differently, and one only needs to look at the members of the EC to see this. The contrast between, for example, the UK and Germany is relatively clear. The UK's economy is centralized, with a dominant stock exchange in London and a great deal of business still based around the capital. In Germany, the dispersed nature of the economy demands a different

[117]

approach — to cater for several stock exchanges and a number of more or less equally sized business centres throughout the country.

An appreciation of the business structure of a country is essential to the public relations professional. Launching an innovative technical product (say in computer networking) in the UK could probably be carried out successfully with (among other things) a consultants' briefing in London. In Germany, however, more than one such briefing, in different cities, would almost certainly be needed to achieve similar impact.

It is worth exploiting these differences in your work where possible. While the 'media tour' is virtually unknown in the UK it is a good way of communicating concepts and technical information elsewhere. The media tour involves senior experts from the company concerned touring major business centres and holding small briefing sessions with the Press. Clearly, this is a tactic worth using in Germany, and it is also widely deployed in North America.

Even within the new Europe, public relations strategies which treat the area as a homogeneous market can run into major problems.

Eastern Europe

In Eastern Europe, the lack of a communication infrastructure, among other things, means a different approach again. Virtually all the public relations 'basics' are missing. There are no reliable press cuttings services, and no journalist listings (for other than political news, etc). In addition, computers, photocopiers, fax machines and reliable telephone services are thin on the ground, while the almost complete lack of any experienced public relations professionals means yet another different approach.

It is necessary either to set up a public relations operation from scratch and train local people or to forge contacts with individual journalists and other professional communicators and then support, educate and manage them from a base where the infrastructure *does* exist. As the Viennese public relations firm PRO&CO pointed out recently: 'Any direct contact between (say) an American industrial giant and the "public relations field" in Hungary or Poland is not very likely to produce the desired results.'

Moving further east, cultural gaps show up even more strongly — the complexities of marketing alcoholic drinks in the Middle East are mirrored in structural (though not religious) terms in the business-to-business field in most countries in the region. Local sponsors, joint ventures and powerful distributors need to be taken into account, as do the variations from state to state. 'Western' business-to-business public relations work, where it is even feasible, needs to take account of each country's commercial and industrial structure to ensure that the often very powerful decision-makers can be targeted accurately and in terms which they understand and appreciate. Local knowledge is essential.

The Far East

Further afield still, Japan has become a hub for international business and yet cultural gaps can still prevent public relations people from operating successfully. Lucy B Siegel, previously director of international affairs for Cosmo Public Relations in Tokyo (and now managing director of the company's New York office) pointed to this in an article in the *Journal of the American Chamber of Commerce* in 1988:

> In Japan, corporate image is everything. Many of the difficulties faced by foreign companies here are traceable to a weak corporate image.
>
> Company image does not carry over from the home market. Yet it is crucial for all aspects of business in Japan — not just for sales, but also for finding business partners, recruiting talented employees and establishing new business relationships. In Japan, a significant part of a company's image consists of demonstrating a long-range commitment to customers and to the Japanese market. This necessitates maintaining a steady flow of information to various audiences . . . Information, not argument, is the guiding force.

[119]

Australasia and North America are much easier to understand in business-to-business public relations terms, but treating the US as a single homogeneous market is almost as foolish as viewing the EC in this way, and the recent growth of ethnic minority businesses adds a further dimension.

RESEARCH

Clearly then, as in any well-run business-to-business public relations programme, research is essential to an understanding of the market conditions in each country requiring public relations support.

What about the competition? The client or company may have four major competitors in the UK, but there may be more in Germany and only one in France. Positioning against the competition cannot be carried out effectively without knowledge of how they communicate, and how they position their products or services. Inappropriate strategies will leave business targets thoroughly unimpressed.

What standards of manufacture and service are required in the relevant countries? Tactical promotion of appropriate standards (such as those produced by the British Standards Institute) can help a public relations campaign enormously, particularly in such fields as electrical products, pharmaceuticals, aerospace and defence systems.

What are the issues affecting the marketplace? Strategies need to take these into account, since promoting speed when the hot topic is flexibility is a bad move, and making price a USP (unique selling proposition) when competitive edge is best gained by concentrating on service back-up is also a poor idea.

MEDIA RELATIONS

In-depth local knowledge of business and trade media is vital if international business-to-business public relations is to be effective. While there are several good international media directories on the market, these can only be used as a starting point.

Constant personnel changes are a fact of life in the media, and it can be the case that the six journalists who confirm their attendance at a technical briefing seminar bear no relation to the names and publications on the original list. Appropriate ways of inviting journalists to your seminars also vary. For example, in continental Europe the more information a journalist receives in the invitation the better, whereas in the UK a 'teaser' approach often works best, since a journalist who feels all the germane information is in the invitation may feel that it is unnecessary to attend. Again, local knowledge is critical to success.

The public relations people 'on the ground' should identify key media and carry out the detailed liaison. In addition, they are in the best position to establish the language requirements both for written matter and presentations. In the business-to-business sector it is often necessary to deal with technical terms and concepts and, unless translation work is carried out correctly, horrendous problems could ensue.

The local public relations people are also in the best position to 'sell' stories and media events to journalists in their territory since they know, for example, which journalists are on which side of any particular industry debate. They are also far more likely to be able to reach appropriate writers; they can more easily identify which ones are strong in particular fields, and have a much better chance of locating the freelance writers who can be very influential in certain industries and countries.

While business, professional and trade titles continue to expand in Europe, there are still far fewer than in the UK and the US. Consequently, readership and circulation tend to be higher, but gaining editorial coverage is correspondingly more difficult.

Guidelines

There are a number of broad guidelines to bear in mind

[121]

when dealing with specific countries. In France, business-to-business publications do not, as a general rule, accept articles prepared by public relations firms although they are interested in story leads from them. Consequently, a well-prepared background information pack, followed up by a letter and phone calls, is the best way to do effective business with the French business and trade media.

In Holland and Belgium, there is a tendency for technical journals to rely on freelance writers rather than staff writers. Therefore, when 'selling-in' stories or promotional ideas, it is important to know which freelancers to contact. If they are interested in what an organization has to say, they will deal directly on its behalf with the appropriate jounal.

The nature and role of publications also differs in other countries. For example, in Germany, Italy and France, there is a broad range of informed general interest publications published on a weekly basis for which there is no equivalent in the UK. If one has a business-to-business story with appeal to a broader readership, publications of this nature are an important additional target group.

In Japan, the press club system, which has no real analogy in the business press in the UK, demands in-depth local knowledge if any progress is to be made at all.

Translation

The importance of language has been touched upon, but it is a subject worthy of more attention than it often receives. Accurate translation is a vital consideration in international business-to-business public relations. Some publications will accept English copy, either because they are published in English or because editorial staff are expected to translate or arrange translation as part of their day-to-day duties. There are many other publications, though, that will not, considering it insulting to have been sent it in the first place. (Imagine yourself as editor of a UK trade publication and receiving a press release and covering letter in Spanish.)

The best approach to language requirements is to check with the local intelligence first, but generally, if the budget is available, translation is advised every time, because it reflects quality, understanding and commitment of approach and increases the likelihood of success. If at all possible, translations should be prepared by a native speaker of the language. While there are many competent UK translation firms, native speakers have a stronger understanding of linguistic idiosyncrasy and nuance, and this is especially important when dealing with technical writing.

Photography and illustration

Creative photography, suitably themed, commissioned and issued to the media, can be of tremendous value in conveying messages about products and services, but when dealing with international work it is important to check that the photography which you have wisely decided to undertake centrally, in order to keep costs to a minimum, is relevant to the foreign markets being addressed. Product shots in which a UK three-point plug is visible will be unlikely to generate a great deal of coverage in countries operating on two-pin plugs.

Do not underestimate the value of illustrations and diagrams to communicate technical concepts. A diagram of a networking system is easy to understand, but the simplicity of the system could be obscured by a translated thousand-word description.

PRINT

Print work can play a major part in an international business-to-business public relations campaign. Good corporate design for print, whether for an annual report, newsletter, technical document, specification sheet or sales brochure, is important, because it enables a company to establish a clear, easily recognizable identity.

Other major considerations include budget control, and an understanding of print-runs, paper sizes and language versions required. As an example, an eight-page, full-colour publication can be very expensive if print-runs in four languages are required. If cost is a restraining factor, as it so often is, a professional solution acceptable to a European readership is to use columns of different languages, or with the appropriate translations on individual pages.

Another useful idea when handling print work is to run a separate language outer cover in black and white or with one colour, with inner pages consisting of colour photography only. This technique enables multi-language versions of the document to be printed cost-effectively, and colour plates do not have to be remade.

MONITORING AND EVALUATION

Research is not only important at the start of a programme, but needs to be revisited at appropriate intervals to take account of changing conditions. Public relations programmes also need careful and constant monitoring to ensure that budgets are not being wasted.

Press cuttings

Press cuttings are often the best way to measure the success of a media-driven public relations campaign. Most industrialized countries have press cuttings companies offering a consistent level of service but, before making arrangements with a cuttings agency, it is vital to check which countries they cover, and what categories of publications they read. This might involve retaining the services of more than one press cuttings agency.

Campaign evaluation

Campaign evaluation should be built into all business-to-business public relations programmes, with activities undertaken and results achieved matched against objectives set at the beginning of the programme. Defining objectives, targets, messages and sensible timescales at the outset is essential, especially since these will vary from country to country.

A good evaluation system will also help in making sure that successful strategies in one market are adapted, where possible, for others and in enabling the public relations professional to kill off those which do not work.

TIME ZONE CONSIDERATIONS

When announcing news internationally, it is important to take time zones into account. For example, it is bad practice to issue news on the East Coast of the US and then think about Europe, because some international media will transmit the American story across the Atlantic and thus pre-empt an orderly release of the information. Nothing is more infuriating to European companies and media than reading a story in the morning papers and then receiving a press release about it the same day.

ELECTRONIC SERVICES

Electronic services have become increasingly easy to use and important as a method of transmitting public relations information to appropriate worldwide destinations. The overall impact of these services — such as fax, electronic mail, international databases and newswire services — has been to speed up public relations communications, so that drafts may be researched, written, approved and issued to the Press in hours rather than days.

The fax is rapidly becoming the standard technology for sending text, technical diagrams and artwork roughs, and is used as an instant postal service. Its role in international business-to-business public relations is vital because it enables the professional to approve complex positioning statements or technical articles very swiftly. Distance is no problem.

Electronic mail is perhaps more sophisticated because it allows text to appear in the destination computer without retyping. This enables public relations practitioners to edit and proof documents very swiftly and efficiently. Although young, e-mail is growing up rapidly, and the next stage of this impressive technology will be the ability to transmit diagrams and artwork easily and cheaply.

International database sources have become very prominent in business-to-business public relations programmes as they provide practitioners with fast and detailed background information. A number of commercial databases are available for interrogation to locate research material, and company and press information. At Infopress, it has been found that the ability to 'keyword search' company, product and issue material around the world without leaving the computer terminal can be invaluable when tracking competitive activity and market conditions. Currently, the US leads the field in terms of the quantity and variety of available databases, closely followed by the UK and Germany.

Newswire services enable public relations firms to send news stories via computer instantly, and also monitor press copy before it is published. This is very important in certain categories of business-to-business public relations, for example when monitoring and responding to particular industry issues in a foreign country or when timing an announcement to coincide with the confirmation of a contract.

EXHIBITIONS

There is now a highly developed trade exhibition industry, and companies marketing to other businesses make use of these to forge business relationships, launch products, locate dealers and distributors, and generally to make news. Press attendance at major trade exhibitions is usually high because journalists can obtain strong news stories quickly. Translated press copy always pays dividents at international exhibitions, and it is worth spending the time to mail appropriate journalists in their native language before and after the event, to increase the impact of news announced at the show.

Among the less obvious points to bear in mind here are those concerned with logistics. Use 'local' public relations practitioners to organize hotels, transport, press invitations, seminar room bookings, hospitality, and press kits. It is also wise to give 'local' people the job of arranging any technical support necessary for demonstrating what might be a complex product. Plan very early if it is felt that the delivery of a paper at the conference running alongside the exhibition would be a good way of communicating concepts and positioning.

Above all, research the exhibition of interest. 'Local' public relations practitioners who have known the exhibition for years will be the best people to ask about the quality of the people who attend in terms of what is required. Participation in foreign exhibitions can be expensive, and as a general rule of thumb it is better to visit such an event and assess its potential before committing major budgets.

Legal restrictions

Before committing budgets to major public relations activity in another country, it is very important to establish whether a proposed programme is legally valid. Legal complications are not as improbable as one might think, particularly when dealing with such things as competitions and sales force incentives. This is another instance where sound advice from local public relations services is invalauble.

USE OF EXTERNAL SERVICES

Central Office of Information

The Government's information service, the Central Office of Information (COI), has a useful overseas service. As part of this, there is a special industrial service set up to handle stories about new products and processes, and provide publicity to trade fairs and trade missions. Additionally, the COI's press service provides news stories, feature articles and other written material for reproduction in newspapers and periodicals abroad, and for briefing purposes.

BBC World Service

Sending stories and information to the BBC World Service is well worth considering as a strategy forming part of an international business-to-business public relations campaign. Broadcasting to 120 million regular listeners in 120 countries, in English and 36 other languages, the BBC World Service has a special export liaison service, which gives manufacturers and service industries an opportunity to influence potential buyers and users.

The BBC World Service will consider new, interesting stories on a wide range of commercial subjects. It broadcasts several business and science-based programmes, and information is best forwarded in a simple, brief format, along with a background note explaining who may be interested in the submission, in which countries, and why.

Department of Trade and Industry

The DTI, through its British Overseas Trade Board and area advisory board, provides a range of commercial services to help exporters establish an industrial and commercial presence in international markets. The diplomatic services' commercial offices and market experts also support the DTI's work in this respect. The DTI can provide useful information on market opportunities, applicable international trade fairs, together with publicity advice including information on technical journals and business-to-business publications, country by country.

Foreign and Commonwealth Office

Her Majesty's Stationery Office (HMSO) publishes The London Diplomatic List which includes London-based embassy staff responsible for press and cultural affairs in their respective countries. These are useful contacts to bear in mind for inclusion on appropriate mailing lists when carrying out an international public relations programme targeting businesses abroad.

CONCLUSION

Marketing products and services to foreign businesses is getting easier all the time, but paradoxically this can make life more difficult for the public relations professional since it increases the amount of competition.

It is wise to begin public relations work abroad by carefully researching the marketplace. Start with the external services mentioned above, then move to electronic 'desk research'. Before writing a strategy plan or even undertaking a relatively simple technical product announcement, it is sensible to talk to 'local' public relations practitioners to ensure an appropriate approach.

Finally — costs. There is a tendency to underestimate the expenditure needed to operate successfully abroad. A public relations programme supporting a machine tool manufacturer in the UK may cost £50,000 a year. To assume that a further budget of £50,000 a year will produce similar impact across Europe is foolhardy when the number of countries involved is considered. Concentrate on priority markets and priority target audiences within those markets. A tightly focused, high-impact project in two countries is likely to be a good deal more valuable than a microscopically thin veneer of promotional effort spread across a whole continent.

CHAPTER EIGHT

The Sponsorship Contribution

DENISE NORMAN

Denise Norman DipCAM, MIPR *has
held senior positions since 1975 in the field
of both national and international sponsorship, involved with both the marketing and
public relations aspects. She comes from a
professional public relations background
and, following general public relations work
with major consultancies, she joined West
Nally in 1971 to head their public relations
division and progressed to an international
group board role.*

*She devised the marketing strategies for
many major international sports events.*

*Following a reorganization in 1986, she
moved into independent consultancy, specializing in international sports and music
events and sponsored TV. Since 1987, she
has been television and marketing director to
the Whitbread Round the World Race. Her
creation of an international TV consortium
for the race, thereby ensuring TV coverage
throughout the world, was a major
achievement.*

The Sponsorship Contribution

Sponsorship is an international calling card which can be used effectively within the global communication and promotional mix. Some of the main benefits to a company/organization of international sponsorship are:

- The company/organization appears to be international. It is a statement of its 'global nature'.

- Sport, music and even environmental sponsorships rarely need translation. They transcend normal language barriers and are enjoyed equally by all those involved, no matter what nationality.

- It is the organization's event/programme and if the organization is lucky enough to have title rights to a global sponsorship, it has an excellent vehicle for promotion, client hospitality, entertainment of opinion formers, staff and dealer incentives, and alerting the business and the news and social columns.

- If the organization cannot have an event/subject all of its own, it can link in with others in a global experience which can make friends, shake hands with governments and develop excellent business-to-business relationships.

- It gives the organization something which matches or enhances its profile and via which contact can be made with its various publics — physically or through TV and other media.

- Opportunities are endless, but selection of the subject is all important for the image and message, and the proposed target publics. It could be a world symphony concert tour in key capitals, or underwriting teaching materials in developing countries.

TARGETING

Every year, there is a wide range of sports events which can be utilized to reach specific audiences. Sports have profiles and an organization can choose those which match their message or purpose. As well as bringing recognition as part of an international club, the use of sport can support a variety of clearly defined marketing and promotional objectives.

It is essential that such objectives are predetermined and they should be part of the total communication package or part of a specific and strategic campaign. For example, if contact with top-level business is required, choose suitable sports — natural choices are golf and tennis — but then hockey, rugby and rowing are also known to have considerable 'business-man appeal'. If a company is looking a bit old and tired, sponsorship of a young, vibrant sport can be part of a new corporate image.

Sponsorship at international level can be expensive but can also be excellent value for money if used properly. Off-the-shelf shopping for a subject is not necessarily the way to go. It is possible to customize and tailor anything from a global rock tour to an environmental campaign — as well as the more traditional sports events.

FINANCE

Olympic and football world cup sponsors are investing

budgets previously reserved for major advertising campaigns. Exclusivity deems each sponsor the biggest and best in its chosen category. It adds 'perceived value' to the name or product and is something which can be an active, major plus to all levels of communication and promotion.

However, for a multi-product Japanese conglomerate, for instance, limited to promoting one of its named products but still for a massive, corporate-style budget investment, these sponsorships become less attractive. Also, TV companies are becoming increasingly wary of major events which make use of them — the medium — at both ends of the financial equation: ie expected to pay for the TV rights and also provide 'free' the exposure of name boards, banners etc from which they get no income.

For the future, it will become normal for sponsors to be involved also with the packaging of TV programming to include their credits and commercials. Organizations will then be able to develop a corporate or product message to link in with their 'in-vision' name exposure.

SPONSORSHIP HISTORY

The Coca-Cola Company regarded as the world's leading sponsor, has utilized sport and music in its 'one-world' message for over 20 years. At national and international level, it supports most of the key events in one way or another. It has a policy of supporting events rather than individual teams or personalities but, as its products diversify, then individual and team support is likely to follow.

Paul Barron, for many years responsible for the company's sponsorship activities, has recorded the campaign considered to be most closely aligned to public relations objectives. It should be noted that the 'excellent public relations benefits' were discovered after the project had been taken on. This is, in fact, often the case with sponsorship activities — the real benefits becoming clear after the investment into 'something good or useful' has been made.

FIFA/Coca-Cola: teaching the world

One of the most successful public relations programmes utilizing sport began in 1976 when the Coca-Cola Company began a long-term sponsorship agreement with FIFA — the world governing body for football.

Dr Joao Havelange, on his appointment as FIFA's president in 1974, made a commitment to step up aid to those countries most in need of football development. Two programmes were devised. An education project to spread football technical expertise as widely as possible and a world youth (under 19) competition to act as a testing ground and showcase for the sport's developing talent.

In 1976, when Coca-Cola became the sole sponsor of these programmes, it was regarded as a minor part of its major commitment to football at the professional and televisual level. In fact, the FIFA/Coca-Cola World Football Development Programme and its subsequent related International Academy, became pillars of the company's public relations efforts globally:

- Coca-Cola's role in these development projects became widely known and acknowledged by national football associations, by government at ministerial level and by the world's media.

- The sponsorship became a dynamic influence on football throughout the world.

- The company's role was seen to give young players from widely differing countries the chance to develop their talents and meet the best players of their age in the world.

- The company was associated with a game that not only increases the individual's sense of fun and enjoyment, but also provokes sporting aspirations closely identified with the growth of countries.

- Strong new relationships were forged by Coca-Cola in many countries with: national governments; leading figures in football; key members of other important sports bodies; television, radio and newspaper organizations; and the public — from the millions who play football to the millions who watch.

- Image-building exposure was achieved for the company's trade name and marks, linked in the media to an important and socially conscious programme.

- Coca-Cola was able to use this sponsorship as part of an advertising campaign and for a product-sampling exercise.

Finally, it established a secure base on which to build future local activities in all the many countries.

MORE HISTORY

Whitbread & Co plc celebrates 250 years in 1992, and has been one of the UK's most ardent sponsors of sport, literary awards and, occasionally, music and art projects. Its only international sponsorship began in 1973 when, with the Royal Naval Sailing Association, it launched the first round the world yacht race to take place. Now one of the biggest international events on the sporting calendar, 'The Whitbread' or 'Le Whitbread' needs no other explanation.

It is right on target with a prime objective for a major sponsorship — the name is the title. Considered one of the greatest challenges left to man (or woman), this race has grown in magnitude and is widely regarded as eclipsing, for many, the America's Cup.

Whitbread is the guardian of a heritage, rather than a solo sponsor, and major corporations from around the world also take part as boat sponsors or as sponsors of or suppliers to the race itself. The close contact between this family of companies and organizations is a prime benefit to all those involved.

The race has ports in the UK, US, Australia, New Zealand and Uruguay, where tourism departments, sports ministries, educational authorities and governments use the race as part of their own promotional activity. To these countries can be added the many more involved with yacht entries in the race: Finland, Sweden, Holland, Italy, France, Germany, Spain, Eire and Switzerland, who have all been regularly involved, and Russia has now joined this list. Each country's diplomats and embassies — as well as overseas business offices — get involved while the Whitbread fleet is in port. Contacts at the highest level are developed. In international business, such contacts are beyond valuation.

The various developing aspects of Whitbread's business — into a wide-ranging owner of fast food groups, quality hotels and country clubs, away from its more traditional 'beer' image — is in line with the race image. It gives a style of endeavour and team work which is likely to appeal to and attract university graduates, as well as giving staff a sense of belonging and pride. To this can be added the availability of an ongoing theme for a wide range of staff and business incentives. High performing employees can be taken to the company's own race stop-over such as Australia for Christmas or Florida for Easter.

There are endless sales promotional themes which can evolve from the race theme and Whitbread customers can all join in, whether collecting vouchers in a Pizza Hut or buying a six-pack of beer in a Threshers off-licence. For the future, new developments are planned. A global clothing and merchandise range, linked to the race and aimed at the international traveller, will take the company name into duty-free shops and major department stores worldwide.

A global educational programme will help teachers to use the high interest in the race as a teaching tool. Pupils' interest in following the yachts' progress around the globe can be used in geography, maths and a whole range of human studies.

The 1973 race started from Portsmouth in the UK with 17 yachts from 6 nations, covered 3 ports, and 14 yachts completed the course. In the fifth race, 1989–90, 23 yachts from 14 countries started, they visited 5 ports, covered 33,000 miles in 9 months, and all but one finished the course.

The race is a fiercely competitive event, considered by skippers and crew alike as the world's toughest ocean race. It is the sailing equivalent to climbing Mount Everest — but is made available to a far greater number of participants. More money, improved technology and a greater national and international excitement have been evident in each race. The support of the media and the development of technology have enabled millions of people to share in the excitement. It is an event which has caught the world's imagination. During the last race, a highly complex telecommunications system could track the yachts' path across the world, receive photographs from on-board and 24-hour contact was maintained.

The Royal Naval Sailing Association has been responsible for the organization since the race's inception with the Whitbread name firmly linked to the event's success and reputation. Each yacht has its own sponsor, sub-sponsors and official suppliers. In addition, Whitbread's own marketing team coordinates the role of Trophy sponsor, with major partners providing technical and financial support, and race sponsors and official suppliers at global and port levels. In the 1989–90 race, it is estimated that US$200 million was invested in The Whitbread.

Like other global events, The Whitbread can work across the normal national boundaries and teach the world about the world. It has proved that mutual understanding between nations — both among the competitors and the sponsors — is a major benefit.

Media interest is very wide and not limited to sport pages as events of global size become hard news as well as being of use across a broad spectrum of general interest publications.

Companies can also use international events as a form of celebration. Whether 25 years old or 250 years, sponsorship of a worthwhile event/subject can be an ideal way of celebrating a birthday. It is contributing something tangible to sport, music or a selected project which can also be enjoyed by all the relevant publics. In Whitbread's case, it celebrates 250 years in 1992 and the *History of The Whitbread Race* in book and TV form make an ideal contribution.

CHAPTER NINE

Internal Communication in a Multinational Organization

MIKE BEARD

Mike Beard MIPR *is director of corporate communications at Taylor Woodrow, the international property, construction, house-building and trading group. He has extensive experience in international corporate and marketing communication obtained in multisite international companies and in consultancy. His in-house experience includes consumer and business-to-business products. He is a former managing director of Burson Marsteller, Singapore. He was elected chairman of the IPR International Committee in 1989.*

Internal Communication in a Multinational Organization

DEFINING THE ACTIVITY

Few business activities can compete with the communication industry in creating a complex terminology and applying it inconsistently. Perhaps this is because communication is often regarded as an art rather than a science. Practitioners today can challenge this assumption as programmes become better researched, structured and monitored, and the diversity of techniques increases.

The staff relations function covers a wide range of programmes, including benefits, working conditions and practices, and training and development. Here, we are examining the employee communication activity which has to be coordinated with all these other aspects of staff relations. This chapter concentrates on some basic principles and techniques and, in particular, how these can be applied in the international arena. Even then, employee communication can be divided into several areas such as legal communication on matters like safety and the communication of personal personnel information.

Most companies have established ways of handling these specialist aspects, often without much influence from the public relations operator. There are strong arguments for good coodination between this specialist communication and the more corporate messages initiated via the public relations route. The former tend to be initiated at national or local level. The major focus here, therefore, has to be on the way an international organization can communicate matters of general interest to its total workforce.

SPECIAL FACTORS IN THE INTERNATIONAL DIMENSION

There is no doubt that people have a great deal in common wherever you operate in the world and so the basic principles of internal communication remain the same. People work better if they know how their tasks are valued and fit into a wider plan. People relate better to managers and supervisors who keep them informed and listen to feedback.

The similarities in human behaviour can be illustrated by the international success of consumer products such as cola drinks and hamburgers. Their products may be the same around the world but companies like Coca-Cola and McDonald's have to translate their presentation and fine-tune it to meet the individual characteristics of local markets. It is an appropriate combination of excellence, consistency and detailed flexibility which plays a major part in determining which consumer products can go international. In the same way, the international communicator must adopt a flexible approach attuned to national differences. There are many special factors which need to be considered and here we can look at some of the more significant aspects.

Language is the first obvious hurdle encountered. Account must be taken of a workforce which may speak French, Urdu or a Chinese dialect. One trap for the unwary is to assume that the Americans, Australians and British share a common language. It is just as important to test communication with other English-speaking markets and modify and translate it if necessary. The general method of dealing with language is to give local managers the responsibility for translating messages originated in English. This may lead to some degree of differing interpretation but is difficult to avoid.

The international arena inevitably adds an extra tier of information to the communication process and creates a sharper challenge on the issue of relevance and interest. No two organizations are the same and much depends on the business and its operating structure. The simplest case might be a company producing a raw material in one country and refining it in another. The most complex situation is the conglomerate operating vastly differing businesses in many countries, perhaps with a complicated organization of national companies and divisional operating structures. This can lead to a wide variety of communication tasks and channels which need to be supported by appropriate communication media.

It is more difficult to reconcile audience interest with corporate objective within a complex international structure. Distance itself is an obvious obstacle to effective communication so corporate communicators have to be quick on their feet and utilize the fast routes now available, such as fax, air courier, and telephone and video conferences.

Where standard materials are being utilized internationally it is vital that the originator is sensitive to local customs and culture, obtained from regular contact with local line management and preferably reinforced by occasional visits to locations. It is also beneficial to become included in the home base visit schedule of overseas management, including both expatriats and overseas nationals. This should help to minimize insensitivities such as the inclusion of scantily dressed women in magazines sent to Muslim countries and references to war-time achievements in materials sent to Germany and Japan. Sadly, such errors are still all too frequent.

It is often the case that an overseas subsidiary has been acquired rather than grown organically. This creates extra communication needs as the international links between the operatives may be shallow in management levels, thus denying full access to the 'grapevine'.

It is most important to take account of legal differences. The first setback could be confiscation of the chairman's keynote video presentation at the point of entry because it has not been cleared properly through local customs regulations. Regulatory requirements can range from the inclusion of a statement in UK reports and accounts to the formal structures of communication on certain issues required in France.

There are many pitfalls, but surmounting them is challenging and rewarding.

RESPONSIBILITY FOR EMPLOYEE COMMUNICATION

It is perhaps worthwhile stating first that employee communication is not the responsibility of an employee communication manager or the trade unions. There was a period, thankfully past, when some companies appointed an employee communication manager and believed that this was the significant step rather than a pointer for the organization. Of course, trade unions are an important element, but as an audience for the company's communication and not as a primary channel for reaching the workforce.

There can be no question that the responsibility rests fairly and squarely with line managers and supervisors. A strong lead and example from the top is the key factor in creating a communication environment. The chairman and chief executive must set the pace and ensure that there is effective communication throughout the organization. Within the management pyramid, there will be both doubters and believers, supervisors with a natural flair and others with none at all.

It is vital, therefore, that communication-skills training is an important element in the management development programme. The employee communication or public relations specialist, acting in a staff role, provides a matrix of communication media and advice on techniques to support line management. Thus, a structure of communication reinforces the effective line manager and provides a safety net for those who are less talented in this area. Sometimes, the role of the corporate communicator is resented because of a confusion about the nature of the role. Line management defines the messages and carries out the personal communication, and the communication specialist provides the specialist support and advice necessary. This will include liaising with other specialists in the organization, particularly in personnel. It should not stop short of frank advice on the quality of information, the way it is received and a detached analysis of the audience reaction.

RESEARCH AND ANALYSIS

A classic approach to public relations policy development indicates that the first stage should be a process of analysis and research, followed by definition of objectives, strategies and action plans. Research is an essential and accepted part of marketing activity and usually accounts for a relatively small part of the total budget. There are established ways of approaching market research and a strong supplier base. The corporate communicator is not so fortunate. The cost of in-depth research can be out of all sensible proportion to the budgets available. Another problem is that there are few off-the-shelf supply options available. Hence, many practitioners focus on cooperative tracking studies such as those organized by MORI in the UK and, sadly, many organizations do little or no research.

These problems are particularly prevalent in researching the internal corporate image where it is obviously impossible to reduce the cost by cooperative activity. Looked at on

[147]

an international basis, the structural problems of obtaining cost-effective research of a mass employee audience are enormous. Consequently, research is generally confined to occasional, expensive in-depth projects. These may never be repeated because of the cost and the adverse management reaction to negative findings! Where the practitioner can get the budget for a major study and, most importantly, a commitment from management to respond positively to the findings, then this will provide a valuable base for policy development.

Many public relations consultancies will offer a 'communication audit' covering the employee audience. There are some arguments, however, for giving this work to a specialist research agency with experience in the field.

Some companies confine themselves to readership surveys of internal publications. These are of limited value because of the random response base and the totally predictable nature of the feedback obtained. Employees inevitably opt for more information, more contact from the centre and more feedback.

Unfortunately, there is normally an incompatible request for a concentration on issues of immediate local interest and concern, underlining the conflict of agendas discussed later. The communicator who works for an organization willing to invest money and substantial management time in regular tracking studies of employee attitudes is indeed fortunate. If this is not available, there are good arguments for relying on the communicator's experience, instinct and a broad base of meetings and regular contacts with middle management and supervision around the international organization. This can be augmented by mini audits in typical locations. It is neccessary to bear in mind that local middle management should be a splendid source of counsel on the communication failings of senior group management but may not be such a reliable source of information about their own performance. As always, the coummunication adviser must provide a detached and objective view of the situation.

[148]

DIFFERING AGENDAS

Inevitably, research will confirm the differing agendas for internal communication which exist between the various levels in a multinational organization. Operatives are most interested in their own work area, the unit, and the plans of local management. There is a small interest in group or divisional matters but, quite naturally, this is largely related to policies and actions which will impact on personal benefits, job security and working practices. Conversely, group management is naturally most interested in motivation of employees to support improved business performance. All successful corporate communication continually recognizes this gap and works to bridge it through balancing and combining plant, national and multinational information and messages. This is often best achieved by injecting corporate information, properly interpreted, into local newsletters, briefing structures and other media.

Another important factor is the difference in levels of understanding and perception of issues between senior management, supervision and the shop floor. Communication advisers who highlight this are sometimes accused by line management of degrading the intelligence of skilled operatives. In fact, the issue is more related to level of interest rather than level of intelligence. Most employees do not choose to read the *Financial Times* or *Die Welt* so attempts by their own management to communicate in these terms have little chance of success. It is necessary, therefore, to keep all communication simple, relevant and interesting.

OBJECTIVES AND PRINCIPLES

Having completed all the background analysis, the international organization needs to define long-term and more immediate objectives for its employee communication programme. Different levels of information need to be added by divisional, national and local management.

[149]

Some objectives will tend to be very general and capable of application to a range of companies in different business areas. Others will be more specific to the particular company and its business activity. Typical general corporate objectives might include:

- recruiting and retaining the best talent;
- motivating employees to achieve their potential and thus optimizing company performance;
- creating a mobile and informed corporate management group.

The strategies through which these and other objectives are pursued might include:

- ensuring that all employees understand the performance needed in their own jobs;
- explaining to employees the way their jobs relate to others in the company;
- communicating the company policies within which employees carry out their own role;
- providing a system of feedback through which employee views and concerns can be conveyed to management.

There is no point in attempting to define standard objectives here. Every company and every situation is different. Specific objectives for a manufacturing company might include:

- communicating fundamental changes in customer needs so that employees understand the need for changes in practices;
- reducing unit labour costs in Europe to levels compatible with alternative manufacturing locations.

Specific methods and actions might include taking employees to product clinics to observe consumer reactions or visits to other manufacturing locations to understand different working practices.

One extra benefit which can accrue to the corporate communicator is from ensuring that company philosophies, business activities and policies are widely understood by employees. The extra impact of a consistent message about the company coming from all levels of international management and employees is a marvellous reinforcement of corporate public relations, advertising and other techniques.

Whatever the objectives of a particular organization, there are some simple principles which have general relevance. The need for a structured approach is key. This requires a process which is defined and understood at all levels. The need for consistency of approach is paramount in creating confidence in the process.

Continuity is also all important. Nothing is more damaging than launching a magazine with a fanfare or instituting a new structure of briefing groups and then allowing it to wither on the vine without explanation or replacement.

It must go without saying that an open and honest approach is vital. Obviously, commercial confidentiality and regulatory and legal considerations can be a constraint to communication. When this is the case, it needs to be explained so that employees trust the integrity of management's approach.

We have seen that messages need to be related to the differing levels of interest. To achieve this, it is best to define simple common messages which can then be expanded for more interested audiences. It is all the better if the expanded information is universally available to all who want it, thus avoiding accusations of two tiers of disclosure.

Some of the key words to be applied therefore are:

- structure;
- consistency;
- continuity;
- honesty;
- simplicity;
- relevance.

One of the most frequent complaints in the past has been that managements only communicate when the news is bad in order to depress employee expectations. A structured and consistent approach minimizes the danger of this reaction.

In developing a company policy, it is important to define what is to be excluded from the corporate employee communication process. For example, salary policy may be excluded because of differing practices in operating countries. Discipline policy may be excluded for the same reason. It is also prudent specifically to exclude individual matters which are resolved through normal management processes.

TEAM BRIEFING — THE KEY FOUNDATION

Whatever media for conveying information are devised, the only sure foundation for successful employee communication is a structure of regular team briefings throughout the organization. Some managers are natural communicators in their everyday style of management. However, a universal and formal structure supplements the good work of the best and provides a framework for managers without a natural gift. Team briefing should be additional to any employee consultation structure which has been formally created within the organization. Of course, the need for team briefing is not specific to multinational companies. Much has been written on this subject. However, it is so fundamental to good employee communication that it is worth touching on some principles.

By team briefing what is meant here is a process by which every employee attends a regular meeting of the operating team to which he belongs, together with the manager or supervisor of that team. It is not sensible to lay down a rigid format. However, a team should usually consist of no more than 12–15 people or the informality is lost and a team spirit becomes more difficult to create and sustain. In large operations, there will be a cascading pyramid of teams beginning with a director and his senior managers. In smaller units, the whole division or department might meet. The only firm principles should be that every employee attends a team meeting regularly and that no team meeting is too large.

Frequency of meetings will vary according to the nature of the team. It is vital that there should be a regular and known cycle and that meetings are only missed in really exceptional circumstances. Once every three months is a sensible minimum although monthly meetings work well. Some units meet weekly to discuss operational matters and cascading communication can be included. When there is a major development an *ad hoc* meeting of the team should be held to cover the issue.

The general style of briefing meetings should be relaxed and informal. All members of the team should be given an opportunity to put items on the agenda in advance as some employees are nervous about raising matters verbally. There should always be an open item on the agenda so that minor concerns can be raised. All contributions to the meeting should be valued and the manager must work to involve everyone in the meeting. An outline agenda for a team briefing session might look something like this:

1. Information about developments at group, national or divisional level.

2. Information about the local unit of which the team is a part.

3. How the team has progressed its tasks since the last meeting.

4. The team's tasks in the period ahead and actions necessary to achieve them.

5. Items placed on the agenda by team members.

6. Any other business — a chance to cover new items and obtain general feedback.

The process is elementary but it does require consistent effort and commitment right through the management chain.

Obviously, there needs to be a system by which group management information is injected into this process. One route is through the communication media such as newsbriefs described in the next section. Another more structured approach followed by some companies begins with the group board meeting. The board can agree during the meeting, or the chairman can define afterwards, what items covered need to be communicated throughout the worldwide organization. A short brief is then passed down the pyramid with additional items added at other levels in the organization. Whichever method or combination of methods is followed, it is important that information should be in writing to ensure that a consistent message is delivered. There are sound arguments for providing all team members with a written copy of the communication, either through the briefing meetings or through other methods such as noticeboards and newsletters.

When team briefing breaks down because of insufficient management commitment then the very foundation of successful employee communication is removed. One effective method for minimizing this risk is to cover team briefing as a specific performance requirement in all appraisals of managers and supervisors.

TECHNIQUES TO CONSIDER

The personal communication through briefing groups and daily contact needs to be augmented by formal communication media. These should be developed according to the particular needs of the organization but we can look at some which are used effectively in a variety of companies.

Newsbriefs

The 'Newsbrief' type of publication is perhaps the most effective tool available for speeding communication in a complex organization. The format is a single sheet newsletter produced on one side of an A4 sheet of paper. It should be produced regularly — perhaps weekly or fortnightly — but with special editions giving immediate information on important news items. A newsbrief should carry short items in easily digestible form on major issues such as policy changes, financial developments, acquisitions, divestments and significant management changes. The publication should be specially tailored to suit noticeboards and briefing groups.

It can be used as the basis for a local site newsletter through the addition of local items to the corporate material from the centre. It is a particularly valuable tool for getting definitive information to overseas locations quickly by the use of fax and telex. The single sheet format is easily distributed and does not present too daunting a translation task to national companies.

Magazines and newspapers

Well-produced publications can play an important part, but in the international area they face the twin challenges of language and relevance. Mixed-language versions rarely work and the local tasks of translation and reprint are usually too daunting, particularly as the time lost in this process reduces topicality. In a multisite operation, it is difficult to give sufficient regular exposure to keep individual locations interested. For these reasons, it is often best to target the publication at international management who ought to share a common language and be able to transfer information into more local communication channels.

Video

This can be a valuable medium for group management to talk briefly to an international audience and, therefore, project their own ideas and personalities. Again, language is the major limitation. The faded voice in original language with translated voice over the top is a clumsy device which seldom works well.

It is often wise to concentrate on a documentary approach and produce this in main language versions at source using native speakers. The personal video message from the chairman can then be aimed at English-speaking managers. The extra complication in video is, of course, the differing television systems in use around the world. It is important to keep a log of all major locations noting their television system.

At least it is now no longer so important to worry about video systems as VHS has emerged as a clear international standard. It would be unwise to rely on local operations to transfer central material from PAL to NTSC for example. This work is best done at the time of the original bulk order.

Employee reports

The production of employee reports covering annual, half-yearly or quarterly financial results and company perfor-mance is now commonplace. These are presented as printed documents, video programmes or a combination of both media. In either case, care must be taken to ensure com-pliance with listing requirements for public companies. Employee reports suffer the same language constraints as other productions so it is important to keep them clear and simple for the mass audience.

Translation is essential if these are the only significant media to be used. It is particularly valuable if local adaptations can incorporate more relevant local performance informa-tion covering national or even unit results.

Apart from video and the printed report, another useful technique is the centrally produced set of slides which give the main highlights in graphic form. These should be accom-panied by a brief script outline to accompany each slide. Thus armed, local managers can make personal presentations to a group of employees, adding unit and departmental informa-tion. The slides can be 35mm or overhead, and it is necessary either to provide translated versions or to include mainly figures and graphics. One technique is to provide English text slides plus an outline to which local management can add translated text. Simple overhead gels can then be produced locally on photocopiers.

[156]

This central briefing pack technique can be adapted to a wide range of communication tasks such as major acquisitions, divestments or organization changes.

Local media

Another effective method of communicating corporate messages internationally is to ensure that they are built into local communication aids which are accepted and effective. This includes getting the information on to local noticeboards, into newsletters and magazines, and also into the local press through carefully targeted distribution of localized versions of corporate announcements.

Translation

When material is being translated for international use, it is obviously essential to provide a high quality translation which is grammatically correct and preserves the original meaning. It is wise to avoid idiomatic English in corporate material intended for international application.

Experience has shown that the most efficient approach to the translation process is to have it executed by a native-speaking professional. Then the translation should be checked by the overseas subsidiary who will be familiar with the nuances of the business and any particular terminology. This route usually provides the best compromise in terms of producing a translation which is accepted by the overseas location and yet creates the minimum local workload.

TWO-WAY COMMUNICATION

Creating an effective two-way flow of communication is the most challenging of tasks. In some cases, there will be formal structures of negotiation or consultation which will facilitate feedback to management on a broad range of issues. Other organizations rely on much less formal processes. In any event, the basic questions which need to be asked are:

1. Is feedback being sought and obtained?

2. Is it being given proper consideration and a response agreed at the right level?

3. Is the response being properly communicated back to the interested employees?

In a formal structure of company consultation, and through briefing groups, issues are raised and answered by local management when they are within their areas of responsibility or are covered by existing briefing papers. A response is obtained from senior management when necessary and communicated clearly and promptly. Where there is general concern about an issue on which a formal position has already been established, then this concern should still be communicated up the management chain.

There are devices which can be used by the corporate communicator to reinforce two-way communication through the structure. When a briefing package or employee video programme is distributed around the organization, it is worth including a feedback report form. This should record the number and location of employees present at the viewing or presentation, the manager responsible, issues raised and answered, and questions outstanding which are referred upwards for a response. Apart from providing a channel for two-way communication, this has the added advantage of providing a monitor demonstrating the depth and breadth of coverage achieved by the particular medium of communication. A high level and coordinated sign-off to all responses is necessary to ensure consistency and to give credibility to the message.

The 'open door' type schemes are worth considering. These resemble suggestion schemes in some respects in that they provide a direct channel for individual employees. A simple standard form is used by the employee to raise questions with management; except for those carefully defined excluded areas such as immediate job responsibilities and personal benefits and career prospects. Personal answers can be sent to employees or less contentious issues can be dealt with through general employee commmunication media.

Whatever devices are instituted to facilitate feedback, there is still no substitute for managers and supervisors 'walking the job' and gaining feedback through an informal and communicative personal style.

INTERNAL COMMUNICATION IN ACTION

Taylor Woodrow is a UK-based company which has created a communication culture over many decades. Teamwork has become so deeply embedded in the organization that words such as 'employee' and 'staff' are never used. Each new recruit is invited to 'join the team'. Since its foundation in 1921, and through its period of internationalization, the company has managed to preserve this distinctive differentiation throughout the organization. Every board agenda contains an item on internal communication.

There are formal consultation processes in businesses employing large numbers of 'team members' and these are complemented by corporate media such as a magazine and regular video programmes. The Taylor Woodrow style is based on a commitment to courtesy, friendliness and an open-door approach to management. The philosophy and approach is explained in detail in a team handbook given to all recruits.

Wiggins Teape is another UK-based multinational company with a strong tradition of effective international employee communication. The group was formerly part of BAT Industries and was floated on the UK Stock Exchange as Wiggins Teape Appleton in 1990.

Wiggins Teape has had a formal procedure on employee communication and has invested in group material to support the structure over many years. During the 1980s, the group management publicly restated its commitment to this activity and instituted a programme to develop and refine publications and briefing packages. The objective was defined as being to:

> . . . stimulate a communicative management style throughout the organization, utilizing effective techniques and media to improve awareness of business objectives and confidence that management is interested in employee concerns.

The company's primary businesses are the international manufacture of a wide range of specialist papers and the ownership of an international merchanting network distributing competitive ranges as well as the group's own products. There is a large number of small and medium-sized manufacturing and distribution sites and several larger operating bases. Two or three hundred employees is a typical average for a site location, although many marketing units are considerably smaller. There is a broad international spread providing typical multinational translation problems for mass employee communication.

One decision taken was to retarget the group magazine and focus on management and supervision while still making it available to all employees. The prime reasons for this change were the language problems and the difficulty in adequately covering local interest subjects in a multisite business. The relaunched magazine concentrated on business and management issues, with the aim of helping to create an international management group well briefed on corporate matters and better able to communicate broadly. In order to reflect the changed objectives, the magazine was given a new look by a leading design consultancy and the quality of writing was adjusted to match an international management audience.

Steps were taken to encourage the widespread use of local site or area newsletters and briefing notes in order to fill any perceived gap resulting from the loss of a mass audience magazine. In reality, anecdotal evidence suggested that less than 5 per cent of shop-floor employees in European countries had bothered to look at a company magazine produced in English with little space to cover local subjects.

The group launched a new one-page, fast-track newsline publication as a means of getting important and interesting information about the group to all units while it was still topical. This news sheet was designed for use on noticeboards and in team briefing sessions. Overseas units were encouraged to translate it and add local items where appropriate.

Wiggins Teape had produced an employee report based on annual results for a number of years. Steps were taken to broaden its appeal by the use of clear visuals and straightforward language. Some operating companies produced their own supplementary reports translated into the main European languages. The process was reinforced by use of video interviews with management, using professional TV presenters, although dubbed language versions were only partly successful because of the stilted effect these produce. Slides and script notes in simple standard form were provided to international management so that these could be used during local presentations on local results and business tasks.

The most innovative element in the total communications approach adopted by Wiggins Teape was the introduction of a 'unit communicator' concept. This was developed because the size and structure of a typical operating unit meant that few were able to justify a full-time public relations officer. Despite this, there was a local unit communication requirement to provide informed advice to management and carry out the staff work on implementing local and corporate programmes. Units were invited to nominate one person, perhaps a personnel officer or a marketing specialist, as their 'unit communicator' to provide feedback to the group on communication issues and to act as a focus for local communication issues.

Group headquarters undertook to provide guidelines, information, advice and support. The suggested responsibilities specific to internal communication were:

1. to assist the centre with local dissemination of group information;

2. to encourage local management to be visible to employees;

3. to provide a link additional to line management between local briefing groups and the corporate affairs department;

4. to assist with setting up and conducting communication audits when appropriate;

5. to increase unit awareness of the benefits of local public relations and community involvement.

The brief for unit communicators included other aspects of corporate affairs, such as local media relations and public affairs programmes. This initiative played a significant part in improving the penetration of good communication practices throughout the widespread international organization. It was backed by a high quality communication guidelines manual designed to assist both line management and unit communicators in implementing group strategies and developing their own programmes.

At the end of the day, however, it must be remembered that the public relations practitioner provides only the backdrop. Success in employee communication ultimately depends on the enthusiasm and hard work of line managers and the lead they get from their Board.

CHAPTER TEN

Raising Awareness of the World Environment

JOHN COLE-MORGAN

John Cole-Morgan BSc (Agric), Dip-CAM, FIPR *is a graduate in agriculture and is especially interested in rural issues and the rural economy. He entered public relations in a post with Spillers Ltd and moved on to a senior public relations position with Fisons Fertilizers Ltd.*

From there, he joined the Civil Service as the first head of public relations to the Agricultural Research Council where one of the exhibitions he arranged won a Prince Philip award.

Later, he became head of public relations to the British Overseas Trade Board and was press officer to HRH The Duke of Kent, Vice Chairman of the Board, for the first Royal visit to the People's Republic of China. While a chief information officer at the Department of Trade, he was given a three-year secondment to set up the public relations department of the British Council.

John now operates as an independent consultant based in Dorset. As a result of both his work and private life, he has travelled extensively in both the developed and developing world.

Raising Awareness of the World Environment

As the world population increases exponentially — having multiplied five times this century — and with 150 extra mouths to feed every minute, the effects of man's activities on the environment are becoming more widely felt. Demands for more resources and land on which to live, for improvements in the standard of living and the consequential increase in release of domestic and industrial waste, are clearly having an adverse effect on the environment at regional, national and global levels. Ever more worrying is the fact that we have no firm basis on which to predict with any certainty what the ultimate effect of our activities will be; we do not know how the earth's systems might alter in response to the changes we are imposing on top of the natural processes of change, and we cannot tell what will be the consequences on human populations. None the less, it is clear that we must act now to correct some of the imbalances which are all too readily apparent. Individuals, commercial organizations and governments throughout the world, not only in the west and north, but in the developing south have to be convinced of this. No public relations programme can ignore this responsibility.

This chapter is not about the mechanics of the world's ecosystems, or the prophecies of gloom and doom. It is about how communication has and can be used to prevent a global catastrophe. At any level, public relations is about changing people's attitudes and there is no doubt that in the last 30 years there has been a signal change in attitude on the part of both governments and individuals to the protection of the global environment, and a growing realization that, unless we change our ways, we could be making life on earth quite literally intolerable.

Who has been responsible for this change? And how was it effected? For it is one of the biggest and fastest shifts in public attitude ever to have taken place. Who, 30 years ago, would have foreseen today's demand for 'green' products? Which major companies were then reserving their glossiest publications to convince their publics that they were environmentally aware? Who would have believed that political parties would be established on a single issue?

Most of the causes of environmental change are rooted in human activities: in agriculture, industry, transport and the very act of breathing. It has long been realized that the way in which man interrelates with his environment is a fascinating and complex matrix of processes. But before the population explosion of the twentieth century, man's influence on his environment was thought to be mainly local in effect and, in global terms, self-buffering. Now, across the world, governments, if they have not already done so, are having to reappraise their attitudes to the environment. Plans covering everything from the disposal of domestic waste to holes in the ozone layer are being produced. Measures to reduce the wasteful use of non-renewable resources and to protect the environment from degradation are high on the agenda of many northern administrations.

Somewhat belatedly, the urgency and magnitude of today's environmental problems have thrust on governments the need to debate and try to resolve issues of a scale and complexity to which they are completely unaccustomed. Politicians, who are much more comfortable dealing with national economic crises, the parameters of which can be fed into Treasury computers, and whose horizons are usually not more than five years, are suddenly faced with trying to resolve priorities on issues which may not seriously affect their electorate during their own lifetime. Is it any wonder that for years many governments tried to diminish the arguments being put to them by environmental lobbyists? For years, our own Ministry of Agriculture, Fisheries and Food and the then Agricultural Research Council tried to paint the now widely accepted organic-farming-promoting Soil Association into a corner full of cranks.

As a young junior executive with one of the UK's major fertilizer manufacturers, I well remember feeling very daring and avant garde, going to the rather shabby offices of the newly formed Friends of the Earth in London to seek out a paper they were said to have published on the effects of nitrates in surface waters. This is an issue which is still troubling the UK's Country Landowners Association, who are seeking assurance that EC directives on the subject will be implemented in a way which minimizes the areas to be designated for restrictions and calls for compensation for losses in income and the capital value of land arising from controls on the use of artificial fertilizers.

There is no doubt that in the late 1960s and early 1970s many people began to feel that there was something wrong and unbalanced about the way man was exploiting his environment. There is equally no doubt that what subsequently took place was a grass roots revolution. It took people with real courage and determination to make the politician stop and listen, and there are many examples of individuals and small groups starting projects and campaigns that have had a major impact. Instead of simply waiting for national or international agencies to act, millions of people began accepting responsibility for the future: joining environmental groups or setting up their own; buying 'greener' products; recycling, particularly bottles, cans and paper; launching community initiatives; and planting trees. They recognized that governments do not have and never will have a monopoly

[167]

on the answers. Nudged, perhaps, by the words of Edmund Burke, the eighteenth century political philosopher who wrote 'nobody made a greater mistake than he who did nothing, because he could only do a little', individuals began making their own contribution; people like Margaret Dinkeldine who, single-handed, started a successful voluntary delittering of Blackheath near London by going out and doing it herself, and shaming others into helping her.

So widespread is the concern today, that in the western and northern world, the prospects of attracting support from individuals, environmental groups and business organizations have never been greater. The cooperation received in the preparation of this chapter from companies and organizations was indicative of their very high level of commitment to awareness of the environment. This is very different from the attitude in the early 1970s, when Friends of the Earth began. In those days, its work was mainly concerned with opposition to established practice and its image was one of long hair and sandals. Today, it is part of the established scene and its work includes proposition as well as opposition. It is widely regarded as an environmental educator of all age groups. Its publications and speakers at events and in schools and colleges serve both to nurture interest in environmental issues and to counterbalance educational drives from commercial interests. Its skill in using both the print and broadcast media to expose environmental malpractice, and to offer solutions, is considerable. Friends of the Earth UK has now earned its colours as an international lobbying organization, pursuing objectives through platforms provided by the EC, United Nations bodies and international trade organizations.

Friends of the Earth UK is a founder member of Friends of the Earth International, the largest international network of organizations campaigning to protect the environment. Founded in 1971, there are now 33 Friends of the Earth International groups worldwide, each group being autonomous with its own operating methods, legal structure and funding base. They are bound together by a common cause: conservation, restoration and rational use of the earth's resources, and their activities are coordinated at an international level through campaigns led by national member groups elected at the Annual General Meeting. These lead groups coordinate political lobbying, citizen action, promotional initiatives and the flow of information through the international network, and are currently concerned with global warming, tropical rain forests, marine conservation, nuclear power and East-West cooperation. Three of the groups are in Eastern Europe and the Soviet Union.

From being considered a fringe body run by anti-establishment people with extreme and alarmist ideas, Friends of the Earth is now a United Nations-accredited, non-governmental organization with observer status at the Food and Agricultural Organization, the International Maritime Organization, the London Dumping Convention, the International Whaling Commission, the Ramsar Convention on Wetlands, and the International Tropical Timber Organization. It has consultative status with the UN Economic and Social Council. Its international secretariat based in London plays a crucial role, facilitating information exchange, joint campaigning and cooperative fund raising, and publishing FOE Link and the FOEI Newsletter. In the UK alone, the turnover of Friends of the Earth is now in the region of about £5 million a year, with the Friends of the Earth Trust, whose major activities are information and educational services, turning over a further £1.5 million, a proportion of which is provided by government and local government sources.

At the other end of the campaigning spectrum is Greenpeace. Started in Canada in 1971, it now has over five million members and offices in 27 countries. Unlike Friends of the Earth, Greenpeace has shunned becoming part of the establishment and will not accept contributions from governments or corporate bodies. All its money is raised by public donation and merchandising. The work of Greenpeace has, until recently, been primarily marine-orientated. It is divided into five campaigning areas: toxics, ocean ecology and wildlife, atmosphere and energy, nuclear weapons control and nuclear disarmament, and, only in the last three years, terrestrial ecology including tropical rain forests and biotechnology. Its maritime activities are coordinated worldwide by the Marine Division in Amsterdam, from which its six ocean-going ships are controlled.

Each year, trustees from the 27 countries meet to decide the year's priorities and while each national office is an independent limited company, the worldwide programme is financed by their pledges towards individual campaigns which may, like the antiproliferation of nuclear weapons campaign, embrace a number of countries over several continents. At the end of each year, the effectiveness of the campaigns are individually assessed in terms of their performance.

Born as a protest movement, Greenpeace has not lost its militant overtones. It still sees non-violent direct action as being a legitimate way of drawing issues to the public attention. Many of its activities, like the use of people in inflatable boats to prevent the dumping of nuclear waste at sea, have called for great personal courage, and the sinking of one of its ships, the Rainbow Warrior, by French agents in Auckland harbour in 1985 was indicative of the level of the French Government's frustration at Greenpeace's endeavours to prevent French nuclear tests in the Pacific.

But, while being admired for its courage, Greenpeace has in the past been legitimately criticized for lack of accuracy and balance in its public statements. Conscious of the damage this was doing to its campaigns with an increasingly knowledgeable and discerning audience, it has, in recent years, appointed respected directors of science to each of its offices and all statements made now have to be cleared through the scientific peer group before issue. Each Greenpeace office has a media director, but its international communication centre based in London coordinates press activities worldwide and controls the activities of dedicated freelance TV crews in every country. The London centre also has the facility to produce video news releases in support of its international activities and a five-person newsdesk issues releases and coordinates public relations activities. Very little is spent on publications.

For quality of publications, it would be hard to beat the old World Wildlife Fund, now renamed the World Wide Fund for Nature or WWF. WWF's support has traditionally come from international establishment figures. Its hallmark is high-quality arguments, top-quality literature, mass orchestration and lobbying of international politicians, all done in the best possible taste. Its endeavours to persuade governments, international agencies, businesses and individuals to take firm and effective action have had resounding success. For example, the work of its Brussels office in public policy development has led to contacts being established with many members of the European Parliament and Commission officials and has helped to ensure that future contracts and legislation drawn up by the EC contain strict environmental protection clauses.

Taking a non-party political approach, WWF works closely with other conservation agencies around the world to influence governments and international bodies to legislate for the protection of the natural environment. To do this, it uses advocacy, campaigning, policy papers, policy analysis and high-level representation. The support it receives from influential world figures like Prince Philip and HRH Prince Bernhard of the Netherlands, as well as leading scientists, businessmen, communicators and economists, are a vital factor in its success.

Until the late 1980s, WWF was not itself involved in conservation, but only with raising money for organizations that were. In recent years, it has, however, developed a more meaningful role as an environmental organization led by conservation work and supported by fund raising. In the last three years, WWF has doubled in size and the focus of its emphasis has switched from the panda to the rain forest. Despite the loss of the panda 'ah!' factor, in 1990 the rain forest appeal raised more money for WWF than any other. Indeed, thanks to record levels of public support, WWF UK was able to contribute more than £7 million towards the cost of the organization's international conservation programme.

[171]

Atomic energy, at one time held out as the most environmentally friendly way of producing electricity, has now proved inordinately expensive first in the UK and then in France, its greatest exponent. Accidents with atomic reactors at Three Mile Island and Chernobyl, and the problem of how safely to store radioactive waste in perpetuity mean that no new atomic power stations are likely to be started in either country until reactors with inherently safer features can be developed and there are better answers to the back end of the fuel cycle. But there is still a need to reprocess spent nuclear fuel.

In the mid 1980s, the label of 'the world's nuclear dustbin' was given to the British Nuclear Fuels Ltd plant at Sellafield. This came to a head after an incident involving radioactive contamination of many miles of the Cumbrian coast. The success of Sellafield in restoring its reputation through an open-information, open-door policy is an important example of communication relating to the world environment. Discarding programmes which explained the benefits of nuclear power, or which put the risks into perspective, Sellafield opted for an open-information policy in which every incident, no matter how minor, was publicized and in which the public was invited to come and see the plant for themselves. Eight million invitations were issued, and a series of five railway trips from all parts of the UK were set up and have been repeated by popular demand. From 29,000 visits in 1985, 160,000 were made in 1989 and Sellafield was declared by the English Tourist Board in 1987 to be the fastest-growing tourist attraction. Between 1988 and 1989, the number of people in Cumbria who said there was no solution to the problem of nuclear waste had fallen from 52 to 35 per cent.

Chemicals underpin our standard of living but the public tends to be in favour of banning them. The public's perception of risk exerts a powerful influence on the chemical industry, especially in terms of product safety and concern for the environment. Fuelled by media scares and real disasters such as Bhopal, and confused by a complex subject area in which there is considerable room for differences of opinion, the public frequently demands unrealistic regulation. 'It is clear that the chemical industry needs more than a quick fix to improve its declining public reputation' warns Guy Liardet, director of public affairs of the Chemical Industries Association (CIA), who believes that much can be done to engender a sense of perspective into the debate by the chemical industry's Responsible Care approach to openness. 'Open attitudes to employees, customers, the public and authorities will stem fear and suspicion' says the CIA.

The concept of Responsible Care was devised and developed by the Canadian Chemical Producers Association originally on a voluntary basis. Its objective was to improve the image of the industry in the eyes of the public and opinion-forming bodies. Responsible Care is now in operation or preparation in at least 10 countries worldwide. Launched in the UK in March 1990, it is a pre-condition of joining the CIA. It requires member companies to give a policy commitment to health, safety and environmental protection as an integral element of business. It has its own logo which can be used by member companies on corporate stationery but not on products or product-related materials.

Environmental debate often suffers from the misconception that industrialists are always biased and environmentalists objective. Prophets of doom attract the headlines; none the less a MORI poll of industrial journalists suggests that there is rising cynicism about whether industries are really attempting to tackle pollution. In his advice to the chemical industry, James Lindheim of Burson Marsteller said that the way in which people analyse risk is irrational and based on emotion. It is therefore pointless, he said, to get into petulantly defensive arguments in a plethora of statistics.

He advised the chemical industry that it needed to echo with sincere sympathy the public concern and to explain what is being done to ameliorate the situation in suitable language. There is no such thing, he said, as a public relations exercise unrelated to actual performance improvements. The industry should always use a spokesperson. When one's image is that of uncaring, faceless impersonal big business, it is quite

[173]

fatal only to issue a statement. The opportunity should not be missed to demonstrate that this business sector is actually peopled with human beings. There are no panaceas, no quick fixes, no solutions by exhortation. The problem must be tackled from the top down through opinion-formers and from the bottom up through the local community. The task of public affairs is a line-management function which affects the bottom line and deserves top-level attention.

The chemical industry giants certainly seem to have taken these messages on board. BASF gives 'a sense of responsibility towards man and environment' and 'open communications with the public and policy makers' as two of its five corporate policy guidelines. Its publication *Environmental Questions and Some Answers* lead the reader through most of the major issues without avoiding the complexities and some issues are further explored in a tape-cassette starring Richard Briers and Penelope Keith.

ICI is equally concerned and recognizes its employees as being the first and most important public in the promotion of its environmental responsibility. The first letter ever directed by the chairman of ICI to every one of its 130,000 employees worldwide was from Sir Denys Henderson outlining the company's environmental objectives. As part of its environmental improvement programme, ICI is, at present, engaged in collating detailed data on its environmental performance on a site-by-site basis and intends making more information available to the public. In 1989, out of £600 million spent on health and safety and the environment, £225 million of that spending was environment-related.

In 1990, British Gas took a series of full-page advertisements in a number of British newspapers to publish 14 excellent and independently written papers on different aspects of the environment debate on which the author of this chapter has drawn freely.

Procter & Gamble's environmental policy dates back to the 1960s when it switched to bio-degradable cleaning materials. Now, through a five-year partnership with WWF, Proctor & Gamble is funding a variety of environmental projects and is building on its environmental programme, which involves improvements to products and packaging, recycling, energy conservation and a commitment to environmental education.

Indeed, more and more commercial companies are recognizing that it makes good business sense to develop products and manufacturing processes that achieve the higher environmental standards society now expects, and even non-manufacturing organizations are vying with each other to show how green they are. In January 1990, the National Westminster Bank published its first environmental review magazine to explain and illustrate to staff and customers the wide range of environment issues the bank faces.

One small but progressive architectural practice, the ECD Partnership (which originally stood for Energy Conscious Design), deploring the small number of buildings designed to a low-energy brief, recently staged an exhibition in London at their own and considerable expense to draw attention to the fact that buildings directly and indirectly were the cause of 50 per cent of the world's carbon dioxide emissions. Their exhibition showed how low-energy design could reduce or even eliminate planetary damage by employing tried and tested methods which were cost-effective. They demanded to know 'why on earth the standards are not universal?'

Much of the credit for this trend must go to a younger generation of managers in many parts of industry and commerce, bringing to their businesses a distinctly different perspective on the importance of environmental issues and insisting that companies carry out environmental audits. The roots of this explosion in environmental consciousness begins in schools, many of which are now carrying out their own 'green' audits, with pupils often setting teachers environmental tests. In a recent survey carried out by KPH Marketing, 56 per cent of UK students said they would take prospective employers' environmental track record into account when considering whether to accept a job offer.

The Green Consumer Guide (Elkington, J. and J. Hailes (1988) Victor Gollancz Ltd, London) which helped launch the 'green' revolution in 1988 has subsequently sold about a

[175]

million copies worldwide and the pressure 'green' consumers have brought to bear on retailers has encouraged most leading supermarket chains to appoint 'green issues' managers or environmental directors to formulate corporate environment policy, and many are now moving on to the next step, insisting that their suppliers develop 'greener' products.

But no matter how much individuals, organizations and corporate bodies do on their own initiatives, governments will always have a crucial role to play in the protection of the environment. The need for more regional, national and international regulations cannot be questioned. Individual responsibility and action can only be sustained within a secure framework of law and, as governments pay more attention to the growth in public concern, a new generation of global laws is appearing, designed to protect the global environment. In developed countries, this may lead to more expensive products and more expensive food and the law makers have to assess not only what is necessary to protect the environment, but how far the consumer, who is pressing environmental issues, is prepared to foot the bill.

At the Montreal Protocol, which held its first meeting in September 1987, 70 nations agreed on measures to reduce the threat to the earth's ozone layer by freezing the use of chlorofluorocarbons at existing levels and aiming to reduce their use by half by 1999. Discussions have started on a plan to control the world's emission of greenhouse gases but the obstacle to international agreement is not finding ways to limit their production, or even assessing what the long-term effects will be; it is the uncertainty of how global warming will affect us. It is believed there could be severe reductions in food production, and people living in low-lying areas like Bangladesh are likely to become even more vulnerable. Ways of saving tropical rain forests are also being looked at and the general ban on whaling is still being fought over between those who feel all whales should be protected and countries with a vested interest in whaling.

In all these issues, governments have responded to the pressure of organizations and individuals, and nowhere more so than in the debate on mining in the Antarctic. In November 1990, the UK Government announced that it no longer rigidly supported the Minerals Convention and was no longer opposed to a mining ban and dropped its objection to designating the Antarctic as a World Park. This, it acknowledges, was the result of public pressure which included thousands of letters to MPs.

WWF's campaign on the Antarctic issue started in the spring of 1990 with a letter from its director, George Medley, to the then Prime Minister, Margaret Thatcher. The campaign gathered pace with a letter-writing campaign to MPs and intensified in the autumn with a nation-wide petition for a world park and a mining ban organized jointly with Greenpeace. As the Prime Minister of Australia, Bob Hawke, put it, 'Ultimately, it is the sheer weight of public opinion that will determine the fate of Antarctica.'

Also as a result of public pressure, decisions at government level resulted in a ban on the ivory trade, which has caused a spectacular drop in the number of elephants killed by poachers. The timber trade in the UK has similarly shown signs of accepting a call to trade only in tropical timber from sustainable forests by 1995.

At a European level, 200 or more environmental directives developed by the European Commission have helped to keep up the pressure on the slowest members of the Community, but the UK's hesitancy is beginning to leave both ordinary members of the public and a growing number of companies feeling uncomfortably exposed. Today, whether one is developing friendships across Europe or selling products in other parts of the Community, the environmental image of one's country counts. No one likes to be associated with the 'dirty man of Europe' image, especially if it means lost sales. The UK's luke-warm support for the EC standards for bathing beaches will inevitably back-fire on many of its holiday resorts.

At a party political level, environmental concerns have been prominent in local and national elections, and the rise of the Green parties has had an inevitable effect on the policies of the main-stream parties. In the UK, membership of 'green' movements jumped from about 1.8 million in 1980 to an estimated 4 million in 1990, and the annual income of the 15 top 'green' organizations, if one includes the National Trust, has been estimated at more than £165 million, a large proportion of which is spent on influencing opinions and changing attitudes. This sort of figure makes the advertising budgets of most companies look puny.

In the UK, the importance of protecting the environment is well covered by the media on an emotional basis, even if the strategic importance is sometimes lost in the rhetoric. But it is in the developing world that much of the real damage is being done and where suffering and deprivation is greatest. Most developing countries do not have the media infrastructure or the sophistication necessary to develop environmental concern in populations which tend to over-use the environment in their struggle to survive. The poor are often driven to mine the environment on a one-off basis; an open wood coke stove is only a tenth as efficient as a gas cooker, but none the less the average American consumes 330 times as much energy as the average Ethiopian. Therefore, if we are serious about the global environment, we must be serious about poverty also, because those in the developing countries are not only unable to foot the bill, but are adding to pollution and waste by inefficient manufacturing and farming processes.

UK support for the United Nations Environmental Programme over the last three years has increased by 320 per cent from £1.25 million in 1988/89 to £4 million in 1991/92. The organization is currently playing a key role in the preparations for the 1992 conference on environment and development. It sponsors a wide variety of plans, programmes, declarations and agreements which provide a framework for global and regional environmental action and can best be described as the environmental conscience of the UN. It aims to motivate and inspire, and to raise the level of environmental action and awareness among all levels of society worldwide. Governed by a council of 58 nations, its decisions are executed and implemented by a secretariat of some 200 professionals, mostly based in its Nairobi headquarters; it is the first UN body to be based in the third world.

Awareness alone will do nothing to alleviate the dangers of our current situation. Governments, international agencies, businesses and individuals have to be motivated into taking firm and effective action. The commitment of thousands of communicators to the various issues affecting the world environment have developed 'awareness'; they must now ensure that action results. The 1992 UN conference on environment and development in Brazil will test the resolve of governments to design and implement the international action necessary to stop current rates of destruction. We must keep on reminding ourselves of the analogy drawn by the American economist, Keith Boulding, who compared the earth flying through space to a space-ship, limited both in its resources and its capacity to absorb waste.

Education, Training and Qualifications Around the World

JON WHITE

Jon White PhDPsych, MIPR *is a public relations practitioner with seventeen years' experience, as an in-house public relations manager, consultant and teacher.*

Organizations he has worked with as a consultant include Legal and General, National Westminster Bank, BP and the Canadian Government's Department of Health and Welfare.

He has headed the Cranfield School of Management's teaching activities in public relations, public affairs and corporate communications since 1986. He holds a PhD in psychology from the London School of Economics and Political Science.

CHAPTER ELEVEN

Education, Training and Qualifications Around the World

Public relations is still a relatively new concern for management, even though its modern origins can be traced to the end of the last century. In, for instance, the UK, which some commentators have suggested is the second most developed centre of practice after the US, senior practitioners believe that the practice is now at the same stage in its development that marketing was in the 1960s (McAvoy, M. (1989) 'Corporate Eyes, Ears and Mouths' *The Economist*, 18 March).

A YOUNG DISCIPLINE

Public relations shows all the signs of being a young discipline. As a Shandwick research report suggested recently, the public relations consultancy market is unstructured, local and early in its growth cycle (Shandwick plc (1990) *The Public Relations Consultancy Market Worldwide 1990*. London). There is not even general agreement about what public relations practice entails. Rex Harlow, in an article which appeared in the *US Public Relations Review* in 1976 (quarterly, Communication

[183]

Research Associates, Inc., Maryland), identified 472 definitions of public relations, which he tried to distil into a working definition.

Debate on the scope of the practice continues. It is still easy enough, in most countries, to move into a career in public relations. There are no barriers to entry, and no specific qualifications are required. The national and international professional associations for public relations practitioners are voluntary associations, and are unable to set firm requirements for entry into practice or enforce standards of practice — even among their own members.

Standards of practice are highly variable. There is a small number of able and respected senior practitioners of public relations around the world, and more highly qualified young people are now pressing to enter the practice and achieving early success in it. But the general standards are not consistently good, or equally developed at all levels, with the result that clients regularly express dissatisfaction about the quality of service they are receiving, or about the standards of practice. Peter Gummer, chairman of Shandwick, which is currently the largest independent public relations consultancy in the world, has suggested that unless the public relations industry worldwide takes urgent steps to improve standards — by recruiting adequately qualified staff and providing proper training to all staff — the industry will not have much of a future (Peter Gummer, address to a meeting of the International Public Relations Association on public relations education and training. London, 21 November 1990).

Education and training are said to be major issues in every country in which public relations is practised. Even in the US, where there are hundreds of public relations courses offered at the university level, criticisms of public relations education are frequently expressed, and senior practitioners raise questions about the value of existing public relations education programmes. The International Public Relations Association (IPRA) has drawn on its international membership to research and recommend standards for public relations education and has published the results of its work in two 'Gold papers' in 1982 and 1990 (IPRA (1982) Gold Paper No. 4, *A Model for Public Relations Education for Professional Practice*, and (1990) Gold Paper No. 7, *Public Relations Education — Recommendations and Standards*).

STATUS OF PUBLIC RELATIONS EDUCATION WORLDWIDE

The IPRA, as a worldwide professional association, is able to carry out regular reviews of the state of public relations education around the world, with the help of members in the 63 countries in which the association has members. A review of education worldwide for the association's meeting in Brussels in June 1990 included reports from 18 countries (Rita Bhimani, Chairman, Education Committee, IPRA, (1990) *The Status of Public Relations Education Worldwide* (Brussels Update)). Full details are available in the review, but the overall impression from the reports — from developed and developing countries — is of growth in interest in public relations education, which is reflected in the willingness of educational institutions and organizations to develop courses and qualifications.

Two examples, one from the country with the most developed offerings for public relations education, the US, and another from a country which has only recently begun to offer education opportunities, Kenya, give an insight into some of the current issues and concerns in public relations education around the world.

In the US, research cited by Professor Don Wright of the University of South Alabama has identified a number of developments in public relations education in the country:

- Enrolments in courses are ahead of employment opportunities for public relations graduates.

- There is a shortage of qualified public relations professors.

- Some practitioners question the abilities of some graduates, and doubt the value of public relations education.

- Public relations education has yet to be accorded the respect given to other professional programmes, such as law and medicine.

- Public relations education may be located in university departments which are inappropriate, such as departments of speech and speech communication.

- Public relations is still not included in university schools of business and management: business faculties know little about public relations and express considerable prejudice against the practice.

- The focus of public relations education needs to be moved away from preparing graduates for entry level jobs, as communication technicians, to preparing graduates for positions that combine public relations administration and management duties with communication skills.

- The development of public relations education can be hindered by the restrictions placed on it by practitioner-orientated professional associations.

- In the US, education appears unable to make a significant contribution to the professional development of practitioners.

- More highly qualified students should be recruited into public relations degree programmes.

- Public relations education receives little support within universities.

- Despite the large number of university programmes in public relations in the US, it is virtually non-existent in the country's major universities.

In Kenya, public relations education has recently been established at the University of Nairobi, to accompany an existing diploma course in practical public relations offered by the Kenya Institute of Management. The country's university course has been initiated with help from the Dutch chapter of the IPRA.

These two examples illustrate some of the current issues in public relations education around the world. The subject is a new one for consideration by academic institutions: it is as little understood in the academic world as it is in the outside world, but it is one that attracts student interest and one that can be established to generate student enrolment. As a new subject, it does not fit easily into other subject categories and, when it is developed within an existing subject area, such as communication or journalism, it is often discounted, and starved of institutional resources and recognition.

When the subject is established in a university setting, it is most often to be found in institutions which — with a few exceptions — use the subject as a means of boosting student enrolment, or which are struggling and looking for new programmes which might attract more students or resources, or which are opportunistic and simply responding to an opportunity to introduce the subject area without any real commitment to it or to treating public relations seriously. The institutions in which the subject is part of the curriculum tend also to be remote from the main centres of public relations practice, or if they are located in main centres of practice, to be institutions which lack academic credibility. As Professor Don Wright pointed out in his survey of US public relations education provision, the most extensive in any country in the world, the subject is virtually non-existent at any of the country's major universities.

Another major problem in public relations education, at the present stage of its development is that it is difficult to find and attract individuals who are sufficiently qualified in terms of educational qualifications — for academic credibility — and in terms of experience of the practice, into teaching. The academically well-qualified practitioner is able to command far higher salary levels in practice than in teaching. Nevertheless some practitioners do choose to move into teaching: younger practitioners because of a commitment to education, and older practitioners for the same reason and because a move into education is a satisfying transition to make towards the end of a career.

Because of the shortage of qualified teachers, the general standard of public relations teaching is poor, with some bright exceptions. In the US, there is a large group of full-time teachers and there are, among this group, some excellent teachers and researchers who are making a definite contribution to knowledge of public relations and its practice, as well as providing excellent instruction to the students who pass through their programmes. Outside the US, there are no groups of teachers of comparable size, and it is difficult to point to known and able teachers in other countries. They can certainly be found, but they are few and far between.

TEACHERS

Teachers of public relations should, according to recommendations made in documents like the IPRA Gold Papers, have practical experience and academic qualifications applicable to public relations practice. Ideally, their qualifications should be at the doctorate level, so that they can carry out and supervise research into practice and contribute to the development of a body of knowledge.

Because doctorates in public relations are not widely available, the faculty will have — if they have doctorates at all — qualifications in other subjects, such as communication or the social sciences. Their original subject interests will determine the view they take of public relations: for example, a faculty member who has pursued studies in communication will tend to see public relations as a form of public or organizational communication, while a former political scientist may view the practice as mediating a number of relationships in which power is a significant factor. This diversity in views of the practice is healthy and is vital to the development of the practice itself, but it does mean that there will be considerable disagreement for some time about the scope and content of public relations practice among academics.

Teachers have to keep in close contact with practitioners. There is general agreement on this point whenever teachers and practitioners meet, and it is a theme of teachers' meetings, such as those held in Europe under the auspices of CERP EDUCATION, the education and research association member of the Confédération Européenne des Relations Publiques (CERP). Close contact is achieved through:

- research carried out by teachers — although there are limits to what can be learnt from questionnaire surveys of practitioners, which sometimes seem to provide the only approach to gathering information about public relations practice;

- work by teachers in consultancies and departments; and

- the collaboration which must take place between practitioners and teachers regarding placements for students.

Teachers do have to contend with scepticism and occasionally prejudice on the part of some practitioners about their role and effectiveness. Scott Cutlip wrote some years ago that 'ignorant anti-intellectualism' is not new in the beginnings of a profession (Cutlip, S.M. (1957) 'The University's Role in Public Relations Education' *Journalism Quarterly* **34** pp 68–73). In public relations, this is expressed by some practitioners who see a gulf between practice and academic discussion of the practice, and believe that the academic has little to contribute to the understanding of practice in the 'real world'.

At the present stage of the development of public relations education, the most effective educators are those who can make the links between teaching and practice. These educators are to be found alongside practitioners in the management of professional associations, such as the Public Relations Society of America (PRSA). They are the researchers whose findings are quoted by practitioners, and the teachers who are able to bring practitioners into their classrooms to add real value to their students' educations.

PUBLIC RELATIONS AND ACADEMIC STUDY

One issue in public relations education which has been addressed in international forums such as CERP Education conferences is whether or not public relations exists as a separate subject for academic study. One view is that it does not. Public relations is a specialized area within a larger discipline, such as management or communication, or it is an example of an applied social science, such as psychology. According to this view, students intending to pursue careers in public relations should first receive an education in the base discipline, with some specialist study to prepare them for work in public relations. The recruitment practices of large consultancies, such as Burson Marsteller in London, support this approach. Graduate entrants to the consultancy are chosen on the basis of the strength of the degree they have taken and its relevance to the consultancy's business goals.

An alternative view is that public relations is a specialist practice, for which entrants should have a specific preparation. This should be given by programmes of study which are interdisciplinary, and draw on the base disciplines of public relations, such as the social sciences, communication studies and management. Programmes such as the four-year degree programmes at Mount Saint Vincent University in Canada and Bournemouth Polytechnic in the UK are examples at the undergraduate level, while Stirling University in Scotland offers a master's programme which is interdisciplinary in approach.

At this point in the development of public relations education, diversity of approach is to be welcomed. It leads to productive argument at conferences and in the pages of professional journals published by organizations such as the IPRA. More importantly, it also means that practitioners can assess the value of a number of models for public relations education.

PATTERN FOR PUBLIC RELATIONS EDUCATION AND TRAINING

By now, the pattern for public relations education and training is becoming clear around the world. Several years ago, the British Public Relations Education Trust (PRET) produced a scheme for education and training which identified the elements required in a programme of education and training for practitioners (PRET (1987) *Scheme for the Education and Training of UK Public Relations Practitioners.* London). The scheme is presented in modified form here, and it draws on conclusions reached at a training conference sponsored by the UK publication *PR WEEK* in September 1987 and a training forum held at the Cranfield School of Management in the UK in March 1987. It also makes use of surveys of professional development needs carried out in the UK, US and Canada in recent years, and documents on career development in public relations produced by the PRSA (PRSA (1979) *Guidebook to a Career in Public Relations.* New York) and the International Association of Business Communicators (IABC).

The PRSA and IABC documents identify a number of levels, or stages, in the development of a career in public relations. At each stage, identified educational and/or training needs must be met, if individuals are to progress to the next stage in their careers and to develop as professionals fully qualified to work in public relations practice. The IABC career development scheme identifies seven levels of professional growth and the skills commonly needed at each level. The PRSA document sets out four career levels which follow from pre-professional academic preparation. These are:

I. Beginning professional
    Introductory training, junior staff, basic skills application.

II. Staff professional
    Junior management. Initial supervisory role.

Basic craftsman, specialist. Follows 18–24 months' experience at level I.

III. Professional manager
Middle management. Directs staff and departmental operations, research, planning, budgeting, personnel, communication and evaluation programmes. Follows at least 5 years' experience at level II.

IV . Senior professional
Top management. Runs public relations operation. Adviser, policy-maker. Has superior knowledge of public relations, public opinion, issues management. Follows up to 10 years' experience at Level III.

The scheme developed in the UK is based on a modified number of levels, set out to include a pre-professional academic preparation or pre-entry stage:

I. Pre-entry: pre-professional academic stage (3 or 4 years).

II. Post-entry: beginning professional stage (years 1 and 2 following entry).

III. Progression to full working level (years 3 to 5 inclusive).

IV. Public relations manager or advanced specialist (year 6 onwards). At this stage, public relations practitioners move on from the full working level and their abilities in project management to manage public relations departments, counsel management at more senior levels, and generally work at a more senior level of management or advanced specialization.

The scheme is modified in this way by findings from a number of Canadian studies which indicate that the beginning of a definite move into either management or advanced specialization occurs at the end of five years in the public relations field. In the US and Canada, accreditation — which recognizes that practitioners have achieved the full working level — is taken after five years of practice and membership in the appropriate professional association (PRSA in the US and the Canadian Public Relations Society in Canada). Results from the Cranfield School of Management's 1987 survey of UK practitioners indicated that the same pattern, showing a move towards management after five years of practice, also applies in the UK.

A scheme which details the education and training requirements of practitioners at each level identified in this four-stage progression also recommends how and by whom these requirements can be met.

I. Pre-entry: pre-professional academic preparation

The *PR WEEK* conference on public relations training in the UK pointed out two routes by which individuals come into the field. The first route involves entry from another career, in journalism, advertising, banking, law or politics, for example. The second route brings individuals into the practice directly from the educational system, as office staff or as graduate entrants.

Prior to entry into public relations practice, 'second career' entrants will have had experience in their other careers (often the reason for their recruitment to public relations positions). As long as this route is open to potential entrants — and there is a strong body of opinion that it should — little can be done to directly influence the experience that these individuals will bring to the practice.

This is not the case with entrants from schools, colleges or universities. With these entrants, some steps can be taken to try to influence the educational preparation they have for work in the field. Increasing numbers of graduates (first degree holders) are presenting themselves for work in public relations. This trend could be assisted by a declaration from professional associations around the world that, by a specified date in the future, preference will be given to potential entrants holding degrees (or equivalent qualifications in countries in which degrees are not commonly available). Schools' career and academic advisers could be informed of this development so that individuals thinking of a career in public relations can be counselled into suitable programmes of study.

Potential entrants into public relations practice should take three or four-year degree or equivalent programmes in one or a combination of the following subject areas: social sciences (political science, economics, sociology, psychology or anthropology), business studies, communication studies, liberal arts or science. Potential entrants should also be encouraged, through university placement offices, talks by representatives of professional associations with student groups, or articles in student publications, to gain practical experience in student politics, journalism, and voluntary or paid employment, which will make them more effective as entrants to public relations practice.

In time, it is likely that a first degree or equivalent qualification aimed directly at fitting graduates for work in public relations will be developed in most of the countries in which it is practised. Professional associations should maintain contact with universities, polytechnics and other institutions to stimulate and shape development of these qualifications. Adequate models for the content of these qualifications can be modified from the experience of universities in the US and Canada and of degree-granting colleges in Australia.

Entry into public relations practice will occur in future, as it does now, through informal approaches made by interested individuals, but professional associations should encourage potential employers to develop graduate entry schemes, drawing on the experience of consultancies and companies now offering these schemes.

II. Beginning professional: post-entry, as graduate or 'second career' entrant

The training requirements are the operation of the practice and the development or refinement of basic skills over a period of two years. At this stage, responsibility for providing training rests primarily with the entrant's employer, but the professional associations should provide guidance to employers on setting up orientation training programmes. They should also provide distance learning materials (videos, booklets, and case study materials) and organize workshops to train trainers involved in orientation programmes as well as on aspects of the programmes themselves.

The orientation should include workshops, directed reading and in-company training dealing with:

- an introduction to public relations practice
- practice in the employing organization
- communication skills
- how businesses and other organizations operate
- introduction to financial management
- media, advertising and marketing
- social research techniques
- an introduction to consulting skills
- project management.

III. Progression to full working level

The training requirement at this level is to develop skills and knowledge, to develop the ability to counsel clients and employers, and to have the skills to recommend, implement and evaluate programmes of action. These skills will include analysis, judgement, communication and research. At this level, practitioners will need to develop abilities to manage programmes and staff. The time period will be three years — from the third to fifth year in practice.

At this stage, it will be the employer's responsibility to make training opportunities available to staff, either in-house or by allowing staff to attend recognized courses. In a number of countries, accreditation — a full membership of national professional associations achieved through examination —

may follow five years of practice. Accreditation in Canada and the US involves submission of a written case study, describing the practitioner's work, and written and oral examinations.

Training should include:

- project and programme management

- organization, social and economic studies

- management: how organizations, staff and financial resources, are managed under routine and non-routine circumstances

- consulting skills

- public relations law and ethics

At this stage, the emphasis in training should be on lessons from practice, on case studies and the experience of practitioners.

IV. Public relations manager or advanced specialist

At this stage, the practitioner needs to develop a knowledge of management or an advanced specialist skill, and abilities to manage or to exercise well-developed specialist skills. It will operate from the sixth year in practice.

Responsibility for personal career development is primarily the individual's, but the individual practitioner should be able to look to his employer for assistance and to national professional associations. Employers and professional associations should stress the need for practitioners at this level to continue to develop their skills, knowledge and ability. Progression to the most senior management levels, or to highly competent advanced specialization will depend on continuing professional development.

Training and continuing professional education will depend at this level on the individual's own career objectives, but work should include:

- management studies (for example, through an MBA programme)

- techniques for bringing about change in organizations
- planning, forecasting and social monitoring techniques
- approaches to business development
- advanced specialist work, for example in the use of communication techniques or in relations with special publics such as governments or investors.

To summarize, this scheme for the education and training of public relations practitioners identifies a pre-entry state and three levels in the development of a career in public relations. It outlines the education and training needs at each of these levels and suggests how responsibilities for meeting these needs can be allocated. Employers, professional associations and individuals all have a part to play in the development of suitable programmes for education and training, which can be developed, country by country to fit into the scheme.

CAREER DEVELOPMENT

A basic scheme can be summarized as follows:

PRE-ENTRY
3–4 years

3–4 year degree programme in one or a combination of the following subject areas: social sciences (including political science, economics, sociology, psychology, anthropology), business communication studies, liberal arts or science.
Experience in employment, student politics or journalism, or voluntary work.

ENTRY
Orientation
2 years

In-company training
Workshops organized by professional associations
Self-directed study

[197]

Progress to full working level (accreditation) 3 years	In-company training Workshops Self-directed study Leading to accreditation or full membership, by examination, of professional associations
Management/ Specialization 2 years and continuing	In-company training Workshops Management courses such as the MBA Self-directed study Advanced specialist training

This scheme sets out elements in a programme of education and training which can be modified for use in differing national circumstances. In some of the developing countries, self-directed study might be an important route to qualification in public relations practice. National professional associations could call on some of the resources available through the IPRA and from some of the institutions now teaching elsewhere in the world for help in the development of study programmes.

The scheme is flexible, and even in a country like the US which has well-established university programmes, allows for a number of routes to qualification for public relations practice.

DEVELOPMENTS FOR THE FUTURE

The recession in a number of the world's major economies at the beginning of the 1990s has brought to an end the period of growth in public relations practice experienced throughout the 1980s. It has had the effect of reducing the numbers of practitioners employed during the boom years. It will have a number of consequences for practice and for education — most of them beneficial.

Some years ago, Professor Jim Grunig of the University of Maryland wrote in his book (Grunig, J. and T. Hunt (1984)

Managing Public Relations, Holt Rinehart and Winston) that the future looked bright for public relations practice, but not necessarily for public relations practitioners. His prophecy has been borne out by recent developments. Public relations, even in times of recession, is now established as a required component of the overall management task. What the recession is doing is forcing companies to dispense with those activities and those staff members whose contribution is questionable. Required public relations activities, and staff educated and trained to carry them out with a high degree of competence, are not threatened by recession.

As the recession at the beginning of the 1990s passes, we can expect to see public relations practitioners as a group, through the leaders of the profession and through their professional associations, become much more aware of the need for well-developed programmes of preparation for practice. More demands will be made of the institutions now offering education programmes, and practitioners will become much more interested in their content. A number of inferior programmes will be swept away by criticism from practitioners, and a number of existing programmes will be improved by practitioner comment and support.

Much more recognition will be given to public relations as a part of management. This will create difficulties for programmes of education based on communication studies or in schools of journalism, because it will be hard for faculties in these programmes to make necessary links with business and management studies programmes.

This is the next task in public relations education. The practice is now served by institutions offering short courses, by colleges and universities providing degrees at the graduate and postgraduate levels, and by a large number of companies which offer training opportunities. In addition, professional associations also offer workshop and seminar programmes. Public relations education now needs to incorporate more business and management content, and to contribute to management training and education.

Some of these developments are already taking place. The newer degree programmes — in the UK, for example, at Bournemouth Polytechnic and Leeds Business School at Leeds Polytechnic — are incorporating more business and management material. Public relations content is finding its way into the curriculum of business schools, but slowly at present. Discussion at the 1990 PRSA conference in New York focused on finding ways to approach the country's business schools to encourage them to include public relations content.

In time, public relations will be accepted as a part of management to be discussed routinely in the same way that marketing or questions of financial management are now dealt with in business and management schools. By the end of the decade, we can expect that public relations practice around the world will be served by a full range of educational and training opportunities:

- As a career option, it will be understood by school leavers, who will also have access to information about programmes of study in public relations.

- Programmes of study will include college and university courses, which will, in most cases, lead to a degree at the graduate or postgraduate level.

- Employers will have properly developed training programmes in place, developed with the guidance of a professional association which will also offer training and educational opportunities and oversee the quality of available training and educational provision.

- Business and management schools, and training companies will offer continuing professional education opportunities, including the MBA and shorter general management training opportunities for practitioners.

Taking Professor Grunig's quote a little further, the future for public relations education is also bright, because much more will be expected of it in the next few years. Public relations is coming of age, as a professional practice, and as an important part of the overall management task. As it does so, it will need the services of well-trained and educated practitioners, who are now being prepared in some of the programmes of education which have recently been established.

Useful Addresses

BBC World Service
Bush House
Strand
London WC2B 4PH
Tel: 071-240 3456

Bournemouth Polytechnic (formerly Dorset Institute)
Poole House
Talbot Campus
Fern Barrow
Dorset BH12 5BB
Tel: 0202 524111

British Association of Industrial Editors (BAIE)
3 Locks Yard
High Street
Sevenoaks
Kent TN13 1LT

British Tourist Authority (BTA)
12 Lower Regent Street
London SW1Y 4PQ
Tel: 071-730 3400

CAM Foundation
Abford House
15 Wilton Road
London SW1V 1NJ
Tel: 071-828 7506

Canadian Public Relations Society (CPRS)
Suite 720
220 Laurier Avenue
W Ottawa K1P 5Z9
Ontario
Canada
Tel: 613 232 122

Central Office of Information (COI)
Hercules Road
London SE1 7DU
Tel: 071-928 2345

Chartered Institute of Marketing
Moor Hall
Cookham
Maidenhead
Berks SL6 9QH

Chemical Industries Association Ltd
Kings Buildings
Smith Square
London SW1P 3JJ

Confédération Européenne des Relations Publiques (CERP)
   (European Public Relations Confederation)
c/o Alvacom
35–41 rue de l'Oasis
F-92800 Puteaux
France
Tel: 33 (1) 47736072

Cranfield School of Management
Cranfield
Bedford
Beds MK43 0AL
Tel: 0234 751122

Department of Trade & Industry (DTI)
1–19 Victoria Street
London SW1H 0ET
Tel: 071-215 5000

Dorset Institute (see Bournemouth Polytechnic)

European Public Relations Confederation (CERP)
see Confédération Européenne des Relations Publiques

Foreign Press Association (FPA)
11 Carlton House Terrace
London SW1Y 5AJ
Tel: 071-930 0445

Friends of the Earth UK
26–28 Underwood Street
London N1 7JQ
Tel: 071-430 1555

Greenpeace
30–31 Islington Green
London N1 8XE
Tel: 071-354 5100

Her Majesty's Stationery Office (HMSO)
51 Nine Elms Road
London SW8 5DR
Tel: 071-873 0011/9090

The Industrial Society (IS)
Robert Hyde House
48 Bryanston Square
London W1H 7LN
Tel: 071-839 4300

The Institute of Public Relations (IPR)
The Old Trading House
15 Northburgh Street
London EC1V 0PR
Tel: 071-253 5151

International Association of Business Communicators
   (IABC)
One Hallidie Plaza, Suite 600
San Francisco CA 94102
USA
Tel: 415 433 3400 (UK: 0621 852310)

International Committee of Public Relations Consultancy
   Associations (ICO)
Willow House
Willow Place
London SW1P 1JH
Tel: 071-223 6026

International Foundation of Public Relations Studies
Interact International Ltd
10a High Street
Tunbridge Wells,
Kent TN1 1UX
Tel: 0892 515222

International Public Relations Association (IPRA)
Case Postale 126
CH-1211 Geneva 20
Switzerland
Tel: 22 791 0550 (UK: 071-306 9000)

[206]

Leeds Polytechnic
Calverly Street
Leeds LS1 3HE
Tel: 0532 832600

Plymouth Marjohn — College of St Mark and St John
Derriford Road
Plymouth PL6 8BH
Tel: 0752 777188

Public Relations Consultants Association (PRCA)
Willow House
Willow Place
London SW1P 1JH
Tel: 071-223 6026

Public Relations Education Trust (PRET)
John Greenall Public Relations
10 Holywell Place
Springfield Meadows
Milton Keynes
Bucks MK6 3LP
Tel: 0908 667664

Public Relations (Journal of The Institute of Public Relations)
68 Purley Bury Avenue
Purley
Surrey CR8 1JD
Tel: 081-660 7495

Public Relations Society of America (PRSA)
33 Irving Place
Union Square
New York NY10003
USA
Tel: 212 995 2230

United Nations Environmental Programme
PO Box 30552
Nairobi
Kenya

University College of Wales
10 Penglais Hill
Aberystwyth
Cardigan SY23 3DB
Tel: 0970 622 691

University of Stirling
Stirling
Scotland FK9 4LA
Tel: 0786 67276

WWF United Kingdom
Panda House
Weyside Park
Godalming
Surrey GU7 1XR
Tel: 0483 426444

Index